Cladding c
Buildings

Cladding of Buildings

Third Edition

Alan Brookes

E & FN SPON

Published by E & FN Spon, an imprint of Routledge, 11 New Fetter Lane,
London EC4P 4EE

Simultaneously published in the USA and Canada by Routledge
29 West 35th Street, New York, NY 10001

First edition © 1985 Construction Press
Second edition © 1993 Construction Press
Third edition © 1998 Alan Brookes

Design by Stephen Cary
Typeset in Gillsans Light by Stephen Cary
Printed and bound in Great Britain by Alden Press, Osney Mead, Oxford

British Library Cataloguing in Publication Data
A catalogue record for this book is available from the British Library

ISBN 0 419 22170 0

Contents

Preface   vii
Acknowledgements   ix
Introduction   I
The frame   I
Knowledge of new materials   2
Principles of jointing   4
Forces moving water through an opening   5
Segmentation of the air space   6
Air seal on inner face   7
Development of 'high tech'   7
References   9

1 Precast concrete cladding   10
Introduction   10
Design guides   12
Standardization and adjustable moulds   14
Types of mould   17
Casting method   18
Tolerances   19
Handling of units during transportation and on site   20
Shape of precast concrete cladding panels   21
Jointing   25
Panel fixings   30
Finishes   33
Weathering   33
References   35

2 Glass-reinforced polyester   36
Introduction   36
GRP production   37
GRP cladding in use   44

Standardization of components   45
Fire resistance   45
Weathering   47
Surface finish   49
Panel stiffening   50
Jointing   53
Thermal expansion   58
Fixings   59
Conclusion   61
References   62

3 Glass-fibre-reinforced cement   64
The material and its advantages   64
Production methods   66
Insulated panels   68
Finishes   69
Performance characteristics   71
Types of cladding   73
Jointing   76
Fixings   78
Panel dimensions and tolerances   80
Handling of units on site and storage   80
Conclusion   82
References and further reading   84

4 Formed metal including profiled metal   85
Forming of metal   85
Profiled metal cladding and roof decking   89
The industry   90
Design guidance   93
Method of manufacture   94

Relevant standards   96
Finishes for metal sheeting   100
Performance criteria   103
Installation   103
References and further reading   112

**5 Sheet metal, composite metal panels,
and rain screens**   113
Introduction   113
Composite metal panels   115
Rolled sheet panels   131
Rain screen panels   133
Finishes   136
Proprietary systems and their fixing   139

Aspect II   140
References and further reading   147

6 Curtain walling — glazing systems   148
Definition   148
Patent glazing   148
Metal box framing   150
Fire resistance   159
Suspended glass assemblies   159
Silicone-bonded glazing   171
Glass   175
References and further reading   176

Index   177

Preface

Since the first publication of *Cladding of Buildings* in 1983, there have been considerable developments in cladding systems and their use in architectural projects. In the main, there has been an increased interest in the use of suspended glazing. M. Stacey (1990) traced the development of suspended glazing from its early use at the Willis Faber Dumas building, Ipswich, by Foster Associates in 1973 through to East Croydon Railway Station (1992), where 12 mm thick glass spanned 3.4 m between fittings supported by cast outriggers. There are now (1996) many types of suspended glazing fittings throughout Europe in addition to Pilkington (Planar) and the RFR fitting from companies including Marcus Summers, MAG, Seele, Eckelt, Vegla, Octatube and SIV (see Chapter 6).

Some of the references included in the early chapters of this book may look a little dated to today's architect. This is partly because of the lack of popularity of some of the materials such as glass-reinforced cement (GRC) and glass-reinforced polyester (GRP) and the consequent lack of development in this field. In contrast, composite metal cladding and suspended glass technology have expanded rapidly in the last decade, and the references in these chapters will seem much fresher to the reader. The reason for leaving in the old references is that continued access to this knowledge base, which is still relevant to the manufacture and use of the materials, may be of assistance both to manufacturers and designers involved in the development of these materials, and may encourage a re-emergence of interest in these types of cladding.

Over the last 10 years architects have shown little interest in GRP and GRC, partly because of the increased cost of the resins and partly because of concerns over weatherability and micro-cracking associated with early formulations of these materials.

Profiled metal cladding has continued to play a part in industrial buildings, and metal composite systems have increased their market share because of the increased speed of erection and greater reliability of the insulation compared with those of built-up systems.

Rain screen cladding and overcladding has also been an important area of development, particularly for applications in high-rise tower blocks, where overcladding offers the opportunity to transform the appearance of the building while improving its thermal performance and durability. There have been some problems with fire performance, and research is still required to optimize the requirements for ventilation within the cavity behind the front skin, taking consideration of the need for fire barriers to reduce fire spread.

Despite the general dissatisfaction with the concrete cladding used on many of the original high-rise blocks of the 1960s and 1970s, the precast manufacturers and, in particular in the UK Trent Concrete, have sustained their share of the cladding market using reconstituted stone cladding.

Increasingly, building has become the collation of factory-made items surrounded by in situ construction. The machine has moved from the building site to the factory. The modern architect thus needs to know the parameters of the manufacturing process and its related quality control procedures in the same way that he or she was traditionally involved in the site process. The trend away from nomination and named specification to performance specification is a mixed blessing in that it further distances the designer from the maker (Stacey, 1991).

The Thames Water Tower, London, which Brookes Stacey Randall Fursdon recently constructed on behalf of Thames Utilities (Slessor, 1995), is an example of greater sophistication in design and construction (Fig. 1). This 18 m high glass tower surrounding a stainless steel core changes in colour responding to barometric pressure variations using sprayed coloured water forming a thin film on the inside face of a toughened glass cylinder. This required time and involvement by the architects in the design and production of the stainless steel support casting and control of the suspended glazing fitting and curved toughened glass to ensure alignment and control of tolerance of the joints, which were critical to the appearance of the building.

This book thus remains essentially a description of the manufacturing processes associated with the six main types of cladding. If architects wish to enlarge their constructional vocabulary, they must relate to and engage in the industrial or manufacturing process. They must also communicate with and gain the trust of those involved in the manufacturing process, and this book is meant to help that dialogue.

As Reyner Banham concluded in *Architecture in the First Machine Age*, architects who propose to run with technology know they will be in fast company, and in order to keep up they may have to discard their whole cultural load, including the professional garments by which they are recognized as architects.

Alan Brookes
London, June 1997

Fig. 1 Thames Water Tower, London (architects: Brookes Stacey Randall Fursdon).

References

Slessor, C. (1995) Public barometer. *Architectural Review*, March.
Stacey, M. (1990) Maximum vision. *Habitat International*, **14** (2/3), 227–233.
Stacey, M. (1991) Design development. *Architects' Journal*, Interbuild Preview, **194** (18), 51–54.

Acknowledgements

The combination of teaching at Oxford Brookes, writing for the architectural press and working as a partner in a busy central London practice needs a careful balance between the specific day to day tasks of a practising Architect and the need to identify the general principles as guidance to others. For assisting me in this balancing act I thank my present partners Michael Stacey and Nik Randall.

For comment and updating of the sections on precast concrete and glass reinforced cement I am indebted to Mike Downing of Trent Concrete and Richard Ferry of Cemfil International. Thanks also to Ulrich Knaack of the Aachen University for his helpful comment on the glazing sections.

Thank you to Anna Grimble who assisted with the typing of this new edition and to Rebecca Allen for preparing the final discs.

Finally, my ongoing debt to my family Jackie, Nicholas, Sarah and James for rubbing off the raw edges of life and assisting me to cope with its conflicting demands.

Alan Brookes
June 1997

Introduction

I find it incredible that there will not be a sweeping revolution in the methods of building during the next century. The erection of a house wall, come to think of it, is an astonishingly tedious and complex business: the final result is exceedingly unsatisfactory.

H. G. Wells (1902)

Non-loadbearing claddings in building, often in panel form, are most commonly used in conjunction with a structural framework. Before considering the six main types of cladding system in detail we should first briefly examine two concepts that have most closely influenced the development of these types of construction.

First, there was the development of frame construction, and second, the introduction of systems of prefabrication, whereby component parts of a building could be fabricated in a builder's yard or workshop prior to their assembly on an actual building site.

The frame

The first building with a skeleton of wrought iron was the Menier chocolate factory near Paris (Fig. 2), built 1871–72, in which the external skin acts purely as a non-loadbearing panel infill. However, it was in Chicago in the latter part of the nineteenth century that the steel-frame building acquired a dominant position in the growth of ideas about panel and frame construction.

The use of the frame offered two main advantages: first, the potential for more square footage per floor area than for masonry construction. As much as one floor in a 10-storey block could be saved by the use of a frame. Second, the whole weight of the building could be carried on the frame, and by reducing the self-weight of the skin the load on the foundations could be reduced.

This combination of advantages led to the intensive development of the Chicago skyscraper, with such examples as the first Leiter building in 1879 and Louis Sullivan's Carson, Pirie, Scott department store of 1899–1904, with its facade of an exposed grid of steel with large glazed infill panels. Subsequent developments led to a position where, as Colin Rowe (1956) commented,

> The frame has been the catalyst of an architecture, but one might notice that it has also become architecture, that contemporary architecture is almost inconceivable in its absence.

Examples of industrialization and prefabrication had occurred all through the nineteenth century, culminating in the spectacular Crystal Palace building for the London Great Exhibition of 1851. Russell (1981) has shown how, following the Battle of Trafalgar in 1805, the mechanized blockmaking plant at the Royal Naval Dockyard at Portsmouth heralded the introduction of machine tools for prefabrication. Herbert (1978), in his excellent study of pioneers of prefabrication, gives an early example in the John Manning portable colonial cottage in 1833, using a timber frame with interchangeable timber panels, all designed for ease of erection. Pressure of prefabrication implied the use of some sort of panel system. Beginning in the twentieth century, prefabrication exploited new techniques and materials. In addition to timber, corrugated metal and cast iron, precast concrete emerged as a new system of building with an enormous potential for prefabrication.

Knowledge of new materials

As early as 1905, J.A. Brodie, city engineer of Liverpool, built a three-storey block of flats using the principle of the 'dovetailed box' with panels cast off site including apertures for doors and windows. Russell (1981) also reports on what must be the first example of sandwich panels in precast concrete at Watergraafseer Garden City, Amsterdam, designed by D. Greiner and built during 1922–24 as part of an experiment to encourage innovative methods in the face of rapidly increasing brick prices. The cladding consisted of an outer layer of concrete, a layer of insulation and an inner layer of lightweight concrete. It may seem surprising, therefore, that the first real guidance on the design of precast concrete was not published until 40 years later (see for example Morris, 1966), when, following the rush to promote and develop housing systems in the 1950s and early 1960s, guidance from the Cement and Concrete Association became widely available. But this is a familiar story in the building industry, where general acceptance of new techniques occurs slowly, and where established texts on building technology tend to be mainly concerned with traditional forms of construction.

Experience has shown that with the use of relatively untried components and techniques, the architect can no longer rely on the traditional means of communication between design and production. In these circumstances architects may have leaned too heavily on manufacturers' expertise in building construction, not realizing that the quality control procedures on site are often insufficient for the site agent to check that the components have been correctly installed.

Fig. 2 Menier chocolate factory.

Changes in the scale of use of materials can create problems of their own. For example, the characteristics of manufacture and behaviour in use of terracotta tiles were well known in Europe at the turn of the century. Even so, failures occurred because of inadequate provision for thermal expansion and contraction processes when such tiles were applied to tall framed buildings in the USA. At such buildings as Atlanta City Hall and the Woolworth building,

New York, the original terracotta has been replaced with another innovative material, precast concrete reinforced with Fibreglass, which itself has also to take account of thermal movement. When specifying new materials we are today able to take advantage of research and development techniques and accelerated testing, and hence predict their performance in use more accurately. Even so, it takes time for the results of this research to filter through into common use. Also, in the building industry it is often difficult to carry out sufficient tests to predict the possibility of failure accurately.

In some cases architects may be wary of using a material because of past experience with similar products. For example, most architects respect the corrosion of metals, and until better means of protection became available there was a general reluctance to use metal panels in building. Thus although techniques for forming or shaping metals were sufficiently well known in 1932 for the development of lightweight metal cladding panels, as used by Jean Prouvé at the Roland Garros Aviation Club building, it was not until much later (Wachsmann, 1961; Sebestyen, 1977) that the principles of design were discussed in detail, and then with little reference to Prouvé.

In general, architects feel a responsibility towards their clients and are reluctant to use a material until it is well tried and tested. This may explain why it was not until the mid-1950s, with the Monsanto 'House of the Future' at Disneyland, that serious investigation of moulded plastics as building panels began, although a survey, published by the *Architects' Journal* (1942), of possible future applications of plastics for the industry reported on building units of comparatively large size being made by a number of moulding methods 10 years earlier. Even so, it was not until conferences such as the one organized by the University of Surrey in 1974 that advice on the design and specification of glass-reinforced polyester (GRP) cladding became more widely available, but 20 years later there are still concerns with the effect of ultraviolet light on certain pigments. Similarly, despite extensive guidance from Pilkington on the use of glass-reinforced cement, there is widespread concern over the performance in use of some of the early formulations.

Changes in use for different building types and markets can also influence architects' attitudes towards a material. Technical guidance on aluminium and steel profiles cladding was hardly thought necessary when its use was restricted to industrial needs. Architects relied entirely on the technical literature produced by the various manufacturers, which although generally very comprehensive did not always show the material in relation to others. It was not until the 1970s that comprehensive guidance to designers on profiled cladding was available from the Central Electricity Generating Board and the Property Services Agency, thanks to the extensive building programme using these materials. Ten years later, British Steel produced their design manual on profiled steel, but interestingly, this did not include manufacturers of composite steel panels with laminated or foamed cores, which were then being widely used. Over the last 10 years there has been rapid development in the design of curtain walling and suspended glazing. The principles of weather resistance using pressure-equalized systems are still not widely understood, and for that reason it has been dealt with in some detail in this book.

Architects and engineers had continued to explore the possibilities of suspended glazing assemblies to take account of the combined action of the glazing and its structural framework. This in turn has led manufacturers to seek ways in which the fittings and fixtures could be designed to take account of the movement within the assembly under wind load.

As yet, there is no established textbook on glazing other than the excellent review of the RFR system as used at Parc de Villette by Peter Rice and Hugh Dutton and my own books of case studies, *Building Envelope* (Brookes and Grech, 1990) and *Connections* (Brookes and Grech, 1992). *Connections* includes our own work using suspended glazing on East Croydon Station (Fig. 3).

Principles of jointing

In any study of cladding it is important that the principles of weather protection are fully understood, as the joints are normally the most critical parts of the assembly.

Thirty-five years ago the Norwegians initiated a scientific investigation into the mechanism of water leakage. Initially they were concerned only with the performance of casement windows, but their investigations subsequently led to a more thorough understanding of the behaviour of the wall itself. Birkeland (1962) published a treatise in which the principles of what was then referred to as the 'rain barrier' and its implications were discussed.

Following the Norwegian studies, scientists at the Canadian National Research Council's Division of Building research institute began similar investigations, and a year after the Norwegian publication a small pamphlet entitled *Rain Penetration and its Control* by Garden (1963) appeared. This publication, in which the terms 'rain screen' and 'rain screen principle' were clearly defined, is still considered to be a prime reference source.

A publication by the Architectural Aluminium Manufacturers Association in the USA (AAMA, 1971) summarizes the principles applied to curtain walling, and makes the point that the terms 'rain screen principle' and 'pressure-equalized design', though closely related, are not strictly synonymous. The rain screen is the outer

Fig. 3 East Croydon Station.

skin or surface of a wall or wall elements backed by an airspace, and so designed that it shields the wall joints from wetting. These principles are described in Anderson and Gill (1988), *Rainscreen Cladding – A Guide to Design Principles and Practice*. The rain screen principle is a principle of design that describes how the penetration of this screen by rainwater may be prevented. The use of pressure-equalized design is an essential part of this principle. Before discussing the application of this principle in detail, it is important to describe how rainwater acts on the surface of a wall.

Forces moving water through an opening

None of the rainwater striking a metal and glass curtain wall is absorbed, as it would be with masonry construction, and a substantial film of water will flow down the surface. If wind is present, the water may also flow laterally or even upwards on parts of the building: the taller the building, the greater will be the accumulated flow over the lower parts of its walls. Lateral flow under wind pressure is greatest near the windward corners of the building, and upward flow is greatest near or at the top of the facade facing the wind. Lateral flow will also be concentrated at vertical irregularities in the wall surface, either projections or depressions, and these may often be joints. In general, the flow of water at vertical joints is much greater than the average flow of water over the wall.

A number of forces then act to move the surface water through any available opening. All of these forces are illustrated schematically in Fig. 4. Probably the most familiar of these is the force of **gravity**, and appropriate methods of counteracting this force are well known. Another force is **kinetic energy**: raindrops may approach the wall's surface with considerable velocity, and their momentum may carry them through any opening of sufficient size. Cover battens, splines or internal baffles can be used to prevent rain entry due to this type of force. A third factor that contributes to leakage is **surface tension**, which gives the water the ability to cling to and flow along soffit areas. The preventive to this action is in the form of a drip at the outer edge of the overhang. Fourth, **capillary action** is likely to occur whenever the space separating two wettable surfaces is small. The way to control water flow by capillarity is to introduce a discontinuity or air gap in the joint that is wider than the capillary path.

It is the next two forces caused by wind action that are the most critical, and the most difficult to combat. **Air currents** may result from differences in

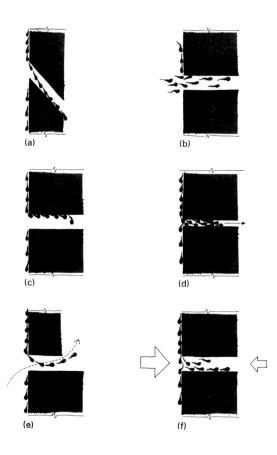

(a)

(b)

(c)

(d)

(e)

(f)

Fig. 4 Forces acting to move water through an opening: (a) gravity; (b) kinetic energy; (c) surface tension; (d) capillary action; (e) air currents; (f) pressure difference (based on AAMA, 1971).

wind pressure over the wall surface, or from convection within wall cavities. These may carry water into the wall. Also, if water is present on one side of an opening and the air pressure on that side is greater than that on the other side, the water will be moved through the opening, no matter how small, in the direction of the pressure drop. This **pressure difference** may be caused by even the gentlest of winds and cause most of the leakage at wall joints.

The conventional approach to combating the last two forces was to attempt to eliminate all openings by using a tight seal, but the more effective and reliable approach is to eliminate the pressure differential across the opening. It is this approach that is known as the **rain screen principle**. The essential features of the rain screen and pressure-equalized wall construction are shown in Fig. 5. Sketch (a) indicates how, with the larger pressure on the outside, water is normally drawn in through the joint. Sketch (b) shows the condition where the pressures on two sides of the outer surface are made equal, thus preventing leakage by gravity, kinetic energy, surface tension or capillary action. Sketch (c) shows how, in order to withstand the effects of air currents and wind pressure, a continuous air space must be provided between the inner and outer skins of the construction.

The pressure-equalized wall consists essentially then of an outer skin (the rain screen) and an inner tight wall with an air space between the two. The pressure equalization is maintained by not tightly sealing the air space with the outside. The seals on the outer skin are known as the **airseals** (Figs 6, 7).

Segmentation of the air space

This is the basic theory. The difficulty in practice is that positive pressures on a facade near the ground are much less than those near the top, and those near the centre of the façade are usually greater than those near the corners. Projecting elements, such as column covers, mullions and transoms, have their effect on the micro-pressures. A horizontal rail may be subjected to pressure at one end and suction at the other. Air flowing through this member trying to equalize the pressure could have a negative pressure at one end, and thus the water would be drawn into its joint. An important requirement therefore in the design of the air chamber is that it should not be a space with a number of widely spaced openings to the outside. Instead it has to be of limited size, subdivided into relatively small areas with ideally one opening in each compartment to the exterior. If mullion or column covers are used as air chambers, they should be blocked off horizontally at height intervals of not more than two storeys to minimize chimney action. Reference should be made to Garden and Dalgleish (1968), who recommend that vertical closures should be provided at each outside corner of the building and at 1.2 m intervals for about 6 m from the corners. Horizontal closures should be used near the top of the wall. Both horizontal and vertical closures should be positioned up to 10 m on centres over the total area of the wall.

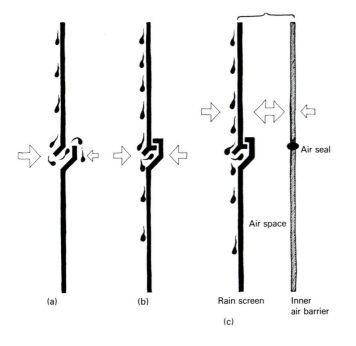

Fig. 5 Essential features of the rain screen and pressure-equalized wall construction (based on AAMA, 1971).

Airseal on inner face

The importance of maintaining the air seal on the inner face cannot be overstressed. Any leakage of air would result in the pressure dropping in the air moved through the gaps to try and equalize the pressure between the air chamber and the inner environment. Another oversight in this respect could be the provision of weepholes in the window sill to allow condensation to pass through. Any such weepholes must be carefully designed to avoid any reduction of air pressure within the chamber. Where openings are provided to the air chamber, they should be large enough to be bridged by water in a heavy rainstorm causing a pressure differential or capillary action.

Development of 'high tech'

'High tech' is a misnomer. It is not a style of architecture as such, but more of an attitude towards design, taking account of and being involved in the process of construction. Technology-led architecture can be seen as a natural development for the Modern Movement in architecture, allowing the use of appropriate technology to inform the designer's intentions. Some authors have identified a thread through Paxton, Prouvé, Gropius, Waschmann, Ehrencrantz, Foster and so on.

The concepts of flexibility and interchangeability, as illustrated by such buildings as Farrell and Grimshaw's Herman Miller factory near Bath (GRP panels), and Foster's Sainsbury's Centre (aluminium panels), have now become an acceptable part of an architect's vocabulary. The serviced-shed approach is increasingly familiar, illustrated by the Reliance Controls factory (Team 10), advanced factory units at Kiln Farm (Milton Keynes architects) and, more recently by the Stratford Market Maintenance Depot, London, 1988, by Chris Wilkinson Architects. Many of these big serviced sheds rely on bright colours, pro-filed panels and exposed structural grids, all posing new methods of jointing and fixing, not covered by established texts on building construction. Archi-tects' demands for brighter colours with contrasting colours for gaskets, window surrounds and flashings have resulted in a need to reconsider the standards of colour matching and finishes of cladding materials.

As new materials and processes are gradually accepted by the architectural profession, manufac-turers respond to an increased demand for these new products and materials by introducing their own pro-prietary solutions onto the market. Under these con-ditions, architects need to make an initial assessment of these systems in order to select the component most suitable for their clients' needs. In order to do this they require a comparative study of the various products to allow them to understand the limita-

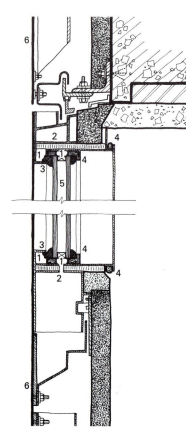

Fig. 6 Pressure-equalized standard wall system (vertical sec-tion): (1) pressure-equalised wall chamber; (2) slotted open-ings; (3) deterrent seal; (4) air seal; (5) hermetically sealed double glazing; (6) spandrel face (based on AAMA, 1971).

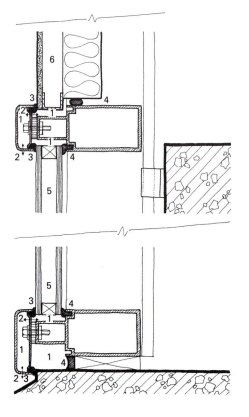

Fig. 7 Sketch detail, pressure-equalized wall: (1) pressure-equalized air chamber; (2) slotted opening; (3) deterrent seal; (4) air seal; (5) hermetically sealed double glazing; (6) spandrel face (based on AAMA, 1971).

tions of the manufacturers' proposals, their performance criteria, finishes and assembly techniques. They need to be able to distinguish between the various jointing solutions available and analyse the weathering characteristics of each cladding material. This book is intended to meet their requirement.

The main theme underlying the following chapters is the method of production of each of the six cladding types discussed. To understand how a material behaves in use it is first necessary to appreciate the processes of its manufacture. Issues such as quality control, cost of production and transportation are fundamental to the proper design of an assembly, and affect decisions on size, shape and finish. The performance of a cladding assembly and particularly its watertightness depends upon its method of jointing; where possible, details are included for each of the applications described. Similarly, the variation in joint size will depend upon the tolerances of construction and the method of fixing used. These are therefore described in detail.

Each chapter contains a description of methods of manufacture, standardization, performance criteria, finishes, durability, jointing, fixing and methods of transportation, storage and erection. There is no particular reason for the order of the chapters other than the fact that precast concrete is arguably the best-known technology, whereas sheet metal and their carrier systems (curtain walling) are the least understood. Glass-reinforced polyester and glass-fibre-reinforced cement tend to be associated with each other, because of the method of their reinforcement, but in fact they are quite different materials, as Chapters 2 and 3 will explain.

Finally, although this book may appear to be about construction, it is also a book about design, for the two are interrelated. It is only through the understanding of technology that the designer can develop design images with confidence. The following chapters summarize the state of the art of cladding technology, and are therefore intended as a contribution towards better design in that field.

References

AAMA (1971) *Aluminium Curtain Walls – The Rain Screen Principle and Pressure Equalization Wall Design*, Architectural Aluminium Manufacturers' Association, New York.

Anderson, J. M. and Gill, J. R. (1988) *Rainscreen Cladding – A Guide to Design Principles and Practice*, CIRIA and Butterworths, London.

Architects' Journal (1942) Future application of plastics. *Architects' Journal*, **29** (10).

Birkeland, O. (1962) *Curtain Walls*, Handbook 11B, Norwegian Building Research Institute, Oslo.

Brookes, A.J. and Grech, C. (1990) *Building Envelope*, Butterworth Architecture, London; Brookes, A.J. and Grech, C. (1992) *Connections*, Butterworth Architecture, London. Republished as one combined volume, *Building Envelope and Connections*, by Architectural Press.

Garden, G. K. (1963) *Rain Penetration and its Control*, Doc CB D0, National Research Council of Canada, Ottawa.

Garden, G. K. and Dalgleish, W. A. (1968) *Influence of Wind Pressures on Joint Performance*, Technical Paper 264, National Research Council of Canada, Ottawa.

Herbert, G. (1978) *Pioneers of Prefabrication – The British Contribution in the Nineteenth Century*, Johns Hopkins University Press, Baltimore and London.

Morris, A. E. J. (1966) *Precast Concrete Cladding*, Fountain Press, London.

Rice, P. E. and Dutton, H. (1995) *Structural Glass*, E. & F. N. Spon, London.

Rowe, C. (1956) The Chicago frame – Chicago's place in the modern movement. *Architectural Review*, **170** (718), 285–289.

Russell, B. (1981) *Building Systems, Industralizations and Architecture*, Wiley, London and New York.

Sebestyen, G. (1977) *Lightweight Building Construction*, George Godwin, London.

Wachsmann, K. (1961) *The Turning Point of Building*, Reinhold, New York.

Wells, H. G. (1902) *Anticipation of the Reactions of Mechanical and Scientific Progress on Human Life and Thought*, Chapman, London.

Precast concrete cladding

Introduction

The main benefits of precast concrete over other cladding materials are its good strength-to-weight ratio, its mobility and, because it is a non-combustible material, its fire performance.

Precast concrete came into its own for use in cladding during the 1950s and early 1960s with the development of high-rise housing. British architects quickly followed the examples of Le Corbusier's Marseilles Unité block, built between 1947 and 1952, although manufacturers such as Trent Concrete and Empire Stone had been manufacturing high-quality cladding elements in the 1920s and 1930s. Morris (1966) has described the history of the development of precast concrete in Great Britain, France and the USA up to 1964. One of the most famous examples is the LCC flats at Roehampton Lane (facing slab manufacturer Modular Concrete), which marks the beginning of the continuous use of concrete cladding in the UK.

Precast concrete has been used for both non-loadbearing and loadbearing cladding units. Both Morris (1966) and the Pre-Stressed Concrete Institute (1973) describe the Police Administration build-

Fig. 1.1 Construction of precast and *in situ* concrete at the Les Espaces d'Abraxas, a monumental housing scheme near Paris (architect: Ricardo Bofill).

ing in Philadelphia, built in 1962, as a major step forward in the structural use of precast concrete wall panels.

The three main advantages of using precast as against *in situ* concrete are:

- speed of erection;
- freedom from shuttering support on site;
- better quality and variety of surface finish, because panels are manufactured in controlled factory situations.

There has been a decline in the use of precast concrete as a cladding material in recent years, attributable to the general dissatisfaction with the high-rise blocks of the 1960s and 1970s. Even so, there have been a number of large projects using non-loadbearing units, such as Vauxhall Cross, London (architect: Terry Farrell); Scottish Office, Leith, Edinburgh (architect: RMJM); Public Records Office, Kew (architect: TBV Consult); and St John's College, Oxford (architects: MacCormac, Jamieson, Prichard). These and other case studies are included in Dawson (1995).

The main manufacturers and fixers of precast concrete cladding – Histon, Tarmac Precast, Marble Mosaic Company, Techcrete and Trent Concrete – form the Architectural Cladding Association.

The economics of precast concrete panel production are a function of standardization of mould shape. Similarly, rationalization of panel size and the means of fixing is important for reducing the cost of transportation and assembly. However, obsession with standardization of mould size and lack of research into applied finishes have hindered development of the variety of size and finish now demanded by the architectural profession.

The industry has relied for too long on the range of finishes possible with aggregates. Much of the precast concrete cladding in the UK is in natural stone, granite or brick. However, times are changing. Examples of more sophisticated finishes from Europe, such as epoxy coating in Holland and Germany, and the work of Ricardo Bofill in Paris and Spain (Fig. 1.1), have shown the exciting possibilities of the material.

Some projects are now being built in the UK that exploit the use of decorative precast concrete units. A recent example is John Outram's work at Sir William Halcrow's pumping station for the London Docklands Development Corporation and the Thames Water Authority, using painted precast concrete fins. These units, manufactured by Diespeker Marble and Terrazzo, are finished in bright colours, using Icosit paint with a clear lacquer top finish (Fig. 1.2). In this case, intricate curves were formed in the timber mould using two 3 mm layers of laminated plywood.

One of the reasons for the previous lack of research by the industry to provide finishes of this type has been the lack of research into the methods of bonding of the finishes to the concrete surface. Developments in penetrating sealer and primers now allow a smooth non-porous surface to the concrete, thus providing a good base onto which the paint coating can be applied.

Design guides

During the 1970s a number of guides were produced to assist the designer to determine the panel size, shape and composition and to select the surface finish in relationship to the appropriate method of casting the panel, many of which are still relevant today. Guides were produced by the Cement and Concrete Association (now the British Cement Association) and the British Precast Concrete Federation.

Useful advice based on American experience

Fig. 1.2 Precast fin units in the manufacturer's yard, painted and awaiting transportation to the LDDC Pumping Station on the Isle of Dogs (architect: John Outram).

was given in the Pre-Stressed Concrete Institute (1973) guide *Architectural Precast Concrete*. Types of finishes related to the method of casting (face up or face down) were covered in articles in the *Architects' Journal* by Michael Gage (23 March 1969), later developed as a book by the Architectural Press (Gage, 1974). Gilchrist Wilson's (1963) *Concrete Facing Slabs* gives examples of surface finishes, using colour illustrations. R. A. Hartland's (1975) book *Design of Precast Concrete* covered all aspects of precast concrete

design, including cladding. Detailing of non-loadbearing precast concrete cladding panels for concrete-framed buildings was also described by Brookes and Yeomans (1981) as part of the *Architects' Journal's* Art of Construction series.

A most useful source of guidance on panel design was produced by the PSA Method of Building Branch (1978) as the result of a comprehensive survey of industry methods by the National Building Agency. This gave guidance on such points as:

- panel types and size limitations;
- panel web thickness;
- design of vertical strengthening ribs;
- removal of moisture from behind panels;
- open drained joints;
- baffle strips, air seals and flashings;
- fixings for panels (cleats and dowels).

A recent publication by the Architectural Cladding Association (Dawson, 1995) updates this information and shows recent case studies of the use of precast concrete. It also includes a good account of the history of architectural concrete.

Standardization and adjustable moulds

Economic use of precast concrete can be achieved only if there is a high degree of standardization in the design of the units. Costs are inevitably higher when greater numbers of panel types are used. There is not only the additional cost of extra moulds, but if moulds have to be continually altered to cast 'specials', the daily casting cycle is disrupted. Moreover, special units require separate stacking and delivery at a particular time. On site, special lifting and erection procedures may be required for non-standard units. The Cement and Concrete Association's (1977) Technical Report No14 gives the main advantages of standardization as follows:

- lower production and erection costs;
- less time for detailing, mould making and production periods;
- reduced risk of detailing and production errors;
- reduced risk of delays due to units being damaged;
- speedier erection.

Architects should therefore make every effort in the early design stages to reduce the number of panel

types. Usually it is easier to standardize panel widths than panel heights, because of the frequent requirement to have different storey heights and parapet levels. In this case it is sometimes possible to adjust the design of the supporting *in situ* concrete frame to avoid the use of non-standard panels (Fig. 1.3). Any additional costs in terms of the shuttering of the main structure can be offset against the savings in greater standardization of precast units. Part of the skill of designing with precast units is this choice between standardizing precast and *in situ* construction. A good example is the student residence for Christ's College, Cambridge (architects: Denys Lasdun & Partners), where the architects have used a basically precast aesthetic *in situ* construction using a limited range of panel forms (Fig. 1.4).

Adjustable moulds

It may also be possible to provide some variety of panel size by adjusting the mould during manufacture. For example, Fig. 1.5 shows an adjustable mould for face-up casting, in which the stop end can be repositioned in the mould. This is more easily done with a panel of uniform thickness than with a coffered panel, where the coffer former will also need to be repositioned. Early consultation with the manufacturer will establish whether or not an adjustable mould is possible for any particular project.

Size of panels

The size of the precast concrete unit is influenced by three factors:

- ease of manufacture;
- method of transportation;
- weight of lifting.

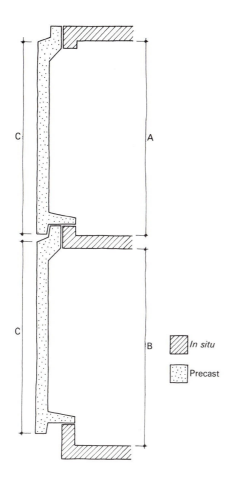

Fig. 1.3 Different storey heights A and B allow standard panel height C.

Fig. 1.4 Student residence for Christ's College, Cambridge (architects: Denys Lasdun & Partners).

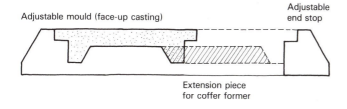

Fig. 1.5 Adjustable mould for a variety of panel sizes.

The width of the unit is related to the method of manufacture, depending upon the type of finish required. For a polished smooth finish the width is restricted to about 1.2 m to allow a man to lean over the unit to polish. Figure 1.6 shows a typical width of unit being polished by hand. If large aggregate is placed by hand, then units should not exceed 2 m in width, unless a moving gantry is used.

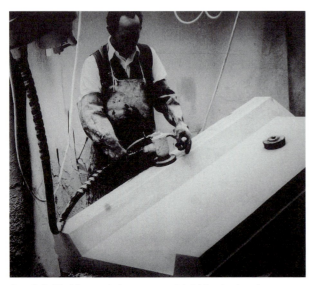

Fig. 1.6 Cladding unit in course of finishing by hand.

Transportation will also limit the size of units. If units are placed flat on a trailer the width is related to payload restriction. There is no restriction on trailers up to 2.895 m (9 ft 6 in) wide. Trailer widths of 2.895–3.500 m (11 ft 6 in) need police permission, and loads exceeding 3.500 m wide need police escort. Thus 1.2–3 m seems to be an economical size for the width of units.

Wider units can be transported on A-frames supported on their long edge. Figure 1.7 shows two methods of transporting units on their edge, where the maximum height when loaded should not exceed 4.880 m. Allowing for the height of the trailer and bearers, panels of up to 4.130 m width are possible. Figure 1.8 shows wall panels being loaded on an A-frame trailer.

Lengths of units are normally 3 × width, and will also be affected by the maximum lengths of the trailers, normally no longer than 12 m. The thickness of the panels is related to the required cover for the

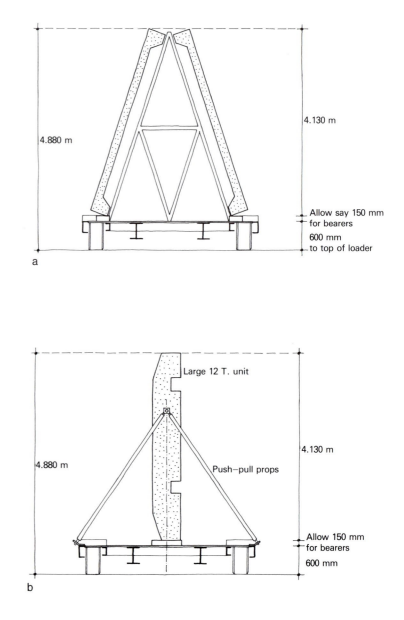

Fig. 1.7 Width of panel related to safe height during transportation: (a) unit transported on A-frames supported on edge; (b) large unit held vertically.

on site. However, some manufacturers have facilities for handling units up to 20 t in weight.

Types of mould

The choice of material for the moulds is usually determined by the number of uses, and is essentially a matter of economics. Thus, although moulds may be made of timber, steel or GRP, there is a considerable cost difference between these materials. Another factor influencing the choice of mould material may be the time taken to make the mould and the rate of output required to meet the erection programme. The shape and size of the units to be cast may also be a consideration.

Timber moulds

Timber moulds are normally used because of their versatility in manufacture. They are certainly the cheapest method for simple panel shapes, with an average of 20–30 castings possible for a complicated panel and 50–60 castings from each mould for a more simple shape. However, they suffer more from wear than steel moulds do, and they do not have the same degree of accuracy. Panels are normally manufactured to BS 8297 : 1995, with a manufacturing variability of ±3 mm. Inaccuracies in bow can be a problem with long units using timber moulds, but these can be reduced by the use of push–pull props (Fig. 1.9). A high standard of finish can be obtained on the moulding by spraying the mould surface with a thin film of GRP.

Steel moulds

Steel moulds offer a better degree of accuracy of manufacture. Also more panels, at least 150 per casting, can be made from the same mould. However, they cost more than timber moulds, and they take

Fig. 1.8 Wall panels being loaded onto A-frame trailer.

reinforcement in the panel web (Fig. 1.18). As a rough guide to deciding the typical thickness of panel related to the longest side of the units, Table 1.1 can be used. Once the panel width, length and thickness have been determined, the cubic volume × the density of concrete will determine the overall weight of the unit.

In most cases wall panels should not exceed 7 t to allow easy handling during manufacture and

Table 1.1 Rule of thumb for panel thickness related to its length	
Panel length (m)	Approximate thickness (mm)
2.0	75 (using stainless steel reinforcement)
3.0	90
4.0	100
5.5	125

longer to make. Steel moulds are usually used only for long runs of absolutely standard units, as they are less easily adjusted than timber moulds.

GRP moulds

Glass-reinforced-polyester moulds, although offering a better standard of accuracy, are more easily damaged and may need frequent repair. Thus the life of the mould is longer than that of timber, but shorter than that of steel. When deeply coffered panels are required, GRP may be cheaper than timber, and also copies of the mould can be made more easily. It will of course be necessary to make the master mould in timber or fibrous plaster to cast the GRP moulds. They are normally used for any unusually shaped or deeply coffered panels. A thin skin of GRP can be used in a timber mould for a better standard of finish (see above).

Casting method

The choice of casting method is normally related to the type of finish required and to the mould table available to the supplier. Three alternative casting methods are normally available for factory production (Fig. 1.10):

- face-up casting;
- face-down casting;
- tilting moulds.

Face-up casting

Face-up casting, although seldom used today, allows various surface finishes to be applied to the top surface while the unit is still in the mould. It is not suitable for tiled finishes or where a smooth surface is required. A disadvantage is that the 'fat' tends to rise to the surface of the concrete, resulting in a weaker face. How-

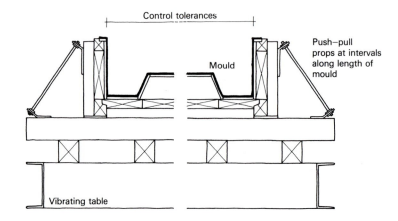

Fig. 1.9 Push–pull props to reduce bowing of timber moulds.

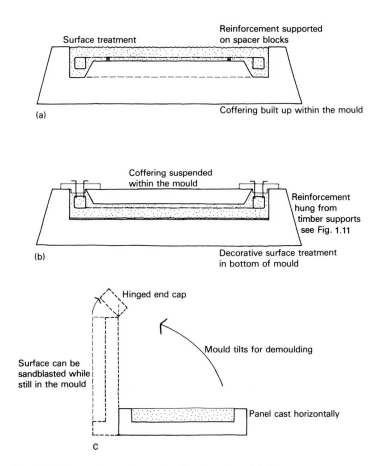

Fig. 1.10 Three alternative methods of casting: (a) face up; (b) face down; (c) tilting moulds.

ever, the reinforcement may be easily supported on spacer blocks without detracting from the external appearance.

Face-down casting

Face-down casting is most suitable for stone veneers, brick, tiles and profiled surfaces. However, if profiled surfaces require a surface treatment, this is done remote from the casting area after the panel has been demoulded. Support of the reinforcement needs attention to ensure adequate cover. Figure 1.11 shows a typical device to control the cover to the reinforcement. Lifting sockets or loops in the back of the panel are easily inserted for demoulding. If these are used, care should be taken to ensure either that they do not interfere with the erection of the panel, or that they are cut off before delivery to site.

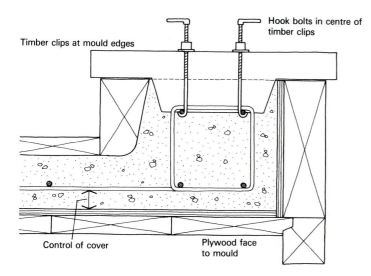

Hook bolts in centre of timber clips

Timber clips at mould edges

Control of cover

Plywood face to mould

Fig. 1.11 Device for controlling cover to reinforcement in face-down casting.

Tilting moulds

Tilting moulds are ideally suited to casting panels of uniform profile. Not all coffered panels can be satisfactorily demoulded. Because handling stresses are less after the panel has been tilted to a vertical position, certain lifting provisions can be omitted and the required quantity of reinforcement for handling can be reduced: in which case the units must be handled vertically during transportation and erection. Thus panels made in tilting moulds are generally thinner than those produced using other casting methods. Care must be taken to ensure that there is adequate reinforcement to resist wind loading when fixed in place.

Tolerances

Three kinds of inaccuracy arise in building: those of manufacture, those of setting out the *in situ* construction, and those of erection of the precast components. BS 8297 : 1995 *Precast concrete cladding (non loadbearing)* gives the permissible deviations of manufacturing inaccuracy on a plus-or-minus basis. Manufacturers prefer to work with deviations ± from the work size, and common practice allows for deviations of ±1.5 mm and ±6 mm depending on panel sizes up to 6 m in length and height. When used in conjunction with *in situ* concrete frame construction with typical deviations of ±15 mm or more, then joints of 5–25 mm between panels can be expected.

In addition to these **induced** deviations, **inherent** movement deviations can also be expected, caused by shrinkage, elastic deformation, creep or changes in thermal and moisture content. A variety of factors influence the extent of these movements, and although not susceptible to precise calculation, generally they are in the order of 1 mm per 3 m

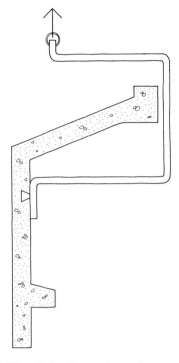

Fig. 1.12 Special lifting device for cranked units.

Fig. 1.13 Special lifting tackle for cranked units.

depending upon the range of temperature expected. These movements are of course reversible, and should be allowed for in the design of fixings.

Handling of units during transportation and on site

Panels require to be lifted from the mould and handled through storage, transportation and finally erection on site. Lifting provision is required in the panels at each stage. One of the main points to consider in the design of precast concrete panels is their weight for handling. Most manufacturers would recommend panels not exceeding 7 t for lifting and 'shuffling' into place on site. This can often place a restriction on the size of the panel, depending upon the density of the concrete used, and the architect must therefore be aware of any weight restriction when determining panel size.

Lifting provision for transportation and erection should if possible be above the centre of gravity, so that when the panel is suspended it will hang in a vertical plane. Tilting of the panels during lifting on site can cause difficulties in placing and fixing. Often it is not possible to suspend a cranked unit, such as a spandrel panel, from its outer face because of difficulties of patching over the fixing sockets. Special lifting devices are then used (Fig. 1.12) to support the panel and keep the centre of gravity below the crane hook (Fig. 1.13).

because of the danger of their becoming unscrewed during lifting. Generally speaking, the shackle device has been found to be the most reliable, but it is expensive. Loops are the most common method. These can be left intact, or burnt off when not required. Collared eyes and shackles are useful for side-hung lifting provision. Clip-on fixings are useful, but the width of hold makes them unsuitable for thin slabs.

Levelling devices

Levelling devices can be used to facilitate panel assembly. They take the form of a cast-in threaded plate and a bolt, which engages in the plate and bears on the floor slab.

Shape of precast concrete cladding panels

The principal types of non-loadbearing panel are storey height and spandrel units (Fig. 1.17). These are either

Fig. 1.14 Tilting platform as used at Liverpool Royal Insurance building.

Panels are often transported horizontally, and require additional reinforcement and lifting provision for handling when lifted into their vertical position. One method of reducing the stress on the panel during such handling is to use a tilting platform (Fig. 1.14). Tight access for crane jibs in relation to the building form should be checked in advance, and allowance should be made for clearance for the jib of the crane above panel fixings (Fig. 1.15).

Fixings for handling are usually loops of reinforcement or cast-in sockets for use with patent lifting devices, which take the form of shackles, stranded steel loops, collared eyes or clip-on bolts. Common proprietary lifting devices are shown in Fig. 1.16. Screw-in lifting devices should not be used singly

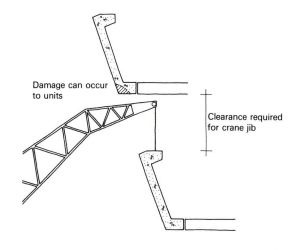

Fig. 1.15 Clearance required for crane jib.

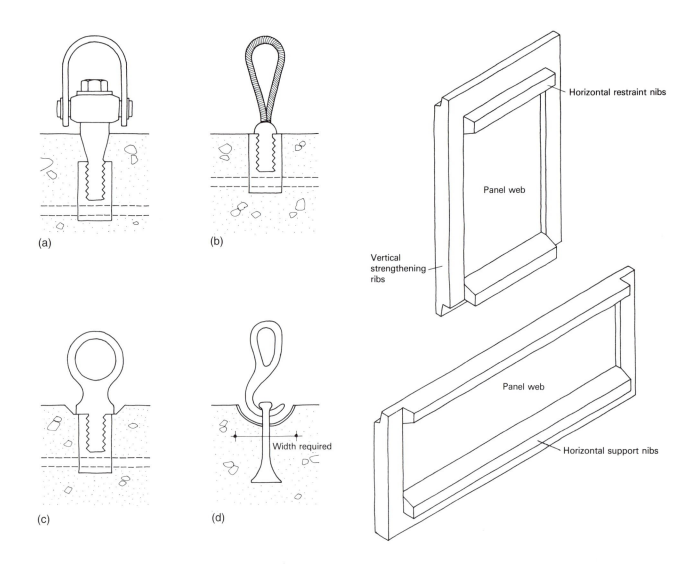

(a)

(b)

(c)

(d)

Width required

Horizontal restraint nibs

Panel web

Vertical strengthening ribs

Panel web

Horizontal support nibs

Fig. 1.16 Principal lifting devices: (a) shackle; (b) loop; (c) collared eye; (d) clip-on.

Fig. 1.17 Strengthening ribs and support nibs on storey height and spandrel units.

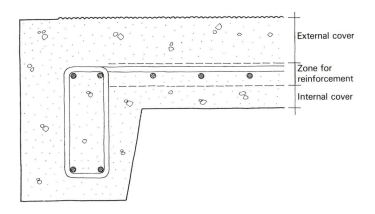

External cover

Zone for reinforcement

Internal cover

	Concrete grade	
	25 N/m²	30 N/m²
External cover	50	40
Reinforcement zone	25	25
Internal cover	25	20
Total depth	100	85

Fig. 1.18 Panel web thickness (mm) related to zone for reinforcement and cover for two types of concrete mix.

of uniform thickness or coffered at their edge to provide a jointing profile. Most panels employ strengthening 'ribs' as beams to transfer dead and vertically applied loads to the structure; the panel 'web' then acts as a slab spanning between these beams.

The shape of the precast concrete cladding units is therefore related to:

—   panel web thickness;
—   horizontal support/restraint nibs;
—   vertical strengthening ribs.

Panel web thickness

Although BS 8297 : 1995 indicates maximum rib spacing and minimum web thickness for coffered panels, in practice the web thickness is governed by the requirements of cover to the reinforcement. This is dependent on the degree of exposure to weather (which BS 8110 : 1985 lists as mild, moderate, severe and very severe), the grade of concrete used (25 N, 30 N/mm²), and whether a facing mix is required to obtain a special finish. Figure 1.18 shows the depths to be allowed for panel web thickness for two types of concrete mix. The thickness of the panel web is determined from the following factors:

—   the external cover to reinforcement;
—   the zone reinforcement;
—   the internal cover to reinforcement.

The depth of external and internal cover should be determined according to the grade of concrete to be used and the conditions of exposure. Normally, external cover is either 40 or 50 mm and internal cover 20 or 25 mm. A zone of 25 mm should be allowed for the reinforcement, stiffening bars and variability of placing the steel in the mould. For most conditions, a nominal thickness of 100 mm can be used for web thickness in design. Using a span : depth ratio of 1:27, the web would then span 2.7 m.

Horizontal support and restraint nibs

The depth of the horizontal support nib is determined from the loadbearing and fixing requirements. The most important consideration is that there should be a minimum bearing of 100 mm on the structural slab plus an allowance of 25 mm for any inaccuracies in the edge of the slab and any danger of spalling. Figure 1.19 shows the minimum dimensions of the horizontal support nib and its bearing upon the type of

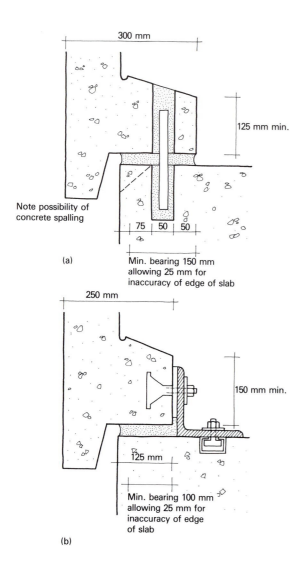

(a)

Note possibility of
concrete spalling

300 mm

125 mm min.

75 | 50 | 50

Min. bearing 150 mm
allowing 25 mm for
inaccuracy of edge of slab

(b)

250 mm

150 mm min.

125 mm

Min. bearing 100 mm
allowing 25 mm for
inaccuracy of edge
of slab

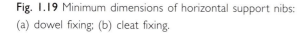

Fig. 1.19 Minimum dimensions of horizontal support nibs:
(a) dowel fixing; (b) cleat fixing.

fixings to be used. Allow for 175 mm with dowel fixings and 125 mm using cleat fixings.

In addition to providing space for reinforcement, the height of the nib is usually affected by the type of fixing used and whether or not it is necessary to provide cast-in fixing sockets. Where an angle cleat fixing is used, the suggested height of nibs is 150 mm. For a dowel fixing, this can be reduced to 125 mm. Concrete corbels and stainless steel bearing angles are extensively used to restrict the height of the gravity support device to fit under raised floors.

Vertical strengthening ribs

The depth of the vertical strengthening ribs is related to the span between the supports, and should be determined from BS 8110 : 1985. For coffered panels the web is designed using a span : depth ratio of 1 : 27, whereas the ribs can be designed as beams with a span : depth ratio of 1 : 17. Sufficient depth is often necessary to accommodate the elements of an open-drained joint (see Figs 1.20 and 1.26), especially where the profile incorporates a drainage groove or where an upstand is provided at the head of the panel. Figure 1.20 shows vertical strengthening ribs of 250 mm to coincide with the depth of a panel needed to incorporate an upstand joint.

The breadth of the rib is governed by such factors as:

- cover to vertical reinforcement;
- the dimensions of columns at panel junctions;
- the accommodation of push–pull sockets for alignment and fixing.

Additional cover will be required if open-drained joint grooves are incorporated in the edge of the panel.

Figure 1.21 shows that for panels abutting columns a breadth of 100–125 mm is normally sufficient, but when the panels occur in front of the structural columns, this may have to be increased to allow for the dimension of the column, so that panel fixing can be within the rib dimension.

Jointing

Sealants

Sealant joints are designed to provide a complete watertight barrier in the form of a single-stage joint positioned towards the panel face. The main types of

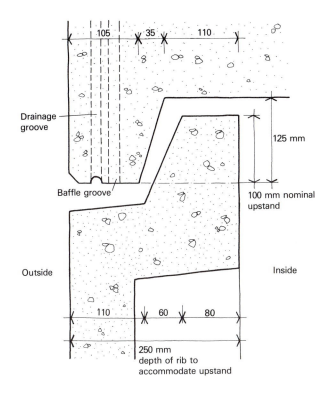

Fig. 1.20 Depth of rib to accommodate upstand at head of panel.

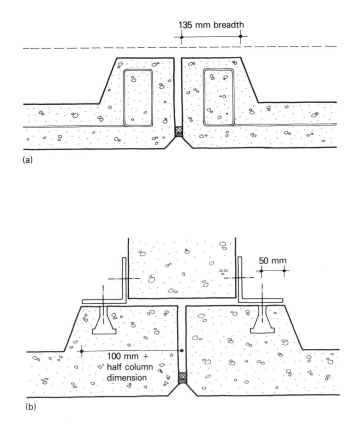

Fig. 1.21 Breadth of vertical strengthening rib related to dimension of column: (a) junction without column; (b) junction with column.

sealant joint for use with concrete cladding are poly-sulphide (one- and two-part) acrylic and low-modulus silicone. Sealant joints are often used for highly pro-filed units such as spandrel or parapet panels.

Two-part polysulphide sealants are most com-monly used because they have good movement capa-bility and thus can offer greater joint size ranges. However, on large jobs with several mixes the colour of sealant can vary, and some manufacturers prefer to use one-part polysulphide, with which the colour is more constant.

Low-modulus silicone (typically Adshead Ratcliffe 1090 or 1099) is used for its good movement capa-bility and longer life expectancy.

Rectangular- or circular-section sealant backing of closed-cell polyethylene foam is used to ensure the correct depth of sealant and to separate it from incompatible materials, which could cause its break-down (Fig. 1.22).

It must be accepted that the sealant joints will need to be repointed during the life of the building, as the proven life of the best sealants is as yet only 20 years. However, sealants in locations protected from the effects of ultraviolet light and extremes of weather may have a greater life expectancy than those in more exposed positions.

Although most cladding manufacturers continue to use sealant joints, possibly because of their ease of detailing, gasket joints can offer a more stable jointing product, particularly when used as a two-stage joint in conjunction with an air seal.

Open-drained joints

The most popular gasket joint is the open-drained baffle joint, first introduced from Scandinavia in the 1950s. With proper detailing, correct specification and con-trol of installation on site, it has proved to be fairly successful. Correct detailing, however, is essential.

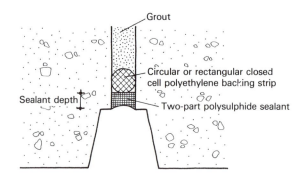

Fig. 1.22 Polyethylene backing strip to ensure correct depth of sealant.

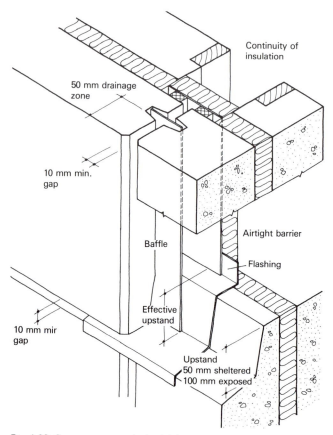

Fig. 1.23 Crossover open-drained joint.

Open-drained joints are explained in BRE Digest No 85 *Joints between concrete wall panels: open drained joints* (BRE, 1967). This covers the principles of and recommendations for details, especially flashings at crossover joints (Fig. 1.23).

The principle of the open-drained joint is to use the geometry of the joint to trap most of the rain in an outer zone and to provide a barrier (air seal) at the back of the joint to prevent air and water (that gets past the baffle) from penetrating into the building. Although the baffle strip acts as a primary barrier to wind-driven rain, the real effectiveness of the joint depends upon maintaining the performance of the air seal. The theory is that, because the seal is positioned at the back of the joint, it is sheltered by the baffle from the ultraviolet light and direct rain, and is subject to less thermal and moisture movement than if it were positioned nearer the face of the panel.

The main elements of the open-drained joint are therefore:

– the baffle strip;
– the baffle groove;
– the air seal;
– an effective upstand at the base of the panel;
– the horizontal flashing at crossover joints.

Baffle strips

Neoprene is the most common material for baffle strips, and is normally used in 50, 63 and 75 mm widths. There are various ways of supporting the baffle strip, including fixing it into plugs in the top surface of the panels. There can be some difficulty in preventing spalling of the concrete using these plugs, and another method devised to facilitate renewal of the baffle is to turn it over a stainless steel pin restrained by bolting through the return ends (Fig. 1.24). The baffle should not be fixed over the pin using staples alone (Fig. 1.25).

Fig. 1.24 Baffle fixed over stainless steel pin for easy renewal.

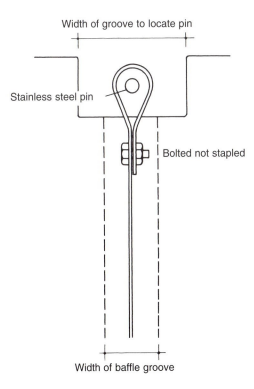

Fig. 1.25 Method of restraining the baffle using a stainless steel pin.

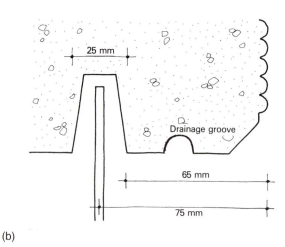

(a)

(b)

Fig. 1.26 Depth of baffle groove from the face of the panel:
(a) without drainage groove; (b) with drainage groove.

The steel pin is located in grooves on either side of the panel joint, which should be wide enough to contain the diameter of the pin (not less than 6 mm) plus two thicknesses of baffle. This will probably be wider than the baffle groove in the side of the panel.

When using baffle strips these should not be stretched before cutting at the base of the panel, otherwise they spring back up the joints, and are then short.

Baffle grooves

Grooves are normally formed by fixing a timber insert to the edge of the mould, and a width of 15–25 mm is normally sufficient to allow a screw fixing and demoulding from the mould. The depth of the groove will vary according to the joint range expected, but 35 mm is normally adequate to accommodate a 75 mm baffle.

The recommended distance of the baffle groove from the front panel is 50 mm, which should be increased to 75 mm if an additional drainage groove is provided (Fig. 1.26).

Air seals

Air seals can be in the form of flexible membranes, gaskets, compressible foam strips and sealants. In practice, this seal has proved difficult to apply. The main difficulty is that of providing a satisfactory air seal at the back of the joint, especially in positions where panels pass in front of floor slabs or where panel joints occur on the centre line of concrete columns. In this case it is not normally possible to apply the seal directly to the back face of the joint.

Upstands

The matching upstand and downstand profile at the horizontal joint is one of the primary features of the open-drained system. The heights of the upstand and downstand are related to the site exposure condi-

Site exposure	A	B
Sheltered	50	75
Moderate	75	100
Severe	100	125

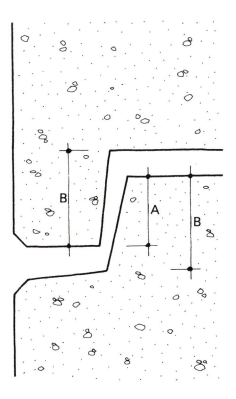

Fig. 1.27 Heights of upstands and downstands (mm). A = effective lap and B = actual lap or downstand.

tions. The effective lap should be 50 mm, and for severe conditions this should be increased to 100 mm (Fig. 1.27).

Flashings

A horizontal flashing must be provided at the junction of horizontal and vertical joints. The principal materials used for flashings are bitumen/polythene or butyl rubber. The width of the flashing should be 300 mm in order to span the vertical joint.

Gasket joints

Although a number of gasket joints have been used, including cellular, tubular, cruciform and fircone gaskets, they all require to be constantly under compression with continuous contact with the panel edge. This is not easy to achieve, because of the variation of joint widths normally attainable on site (typically 10–30 mm). The possibility of blowholes and other unevenness on the concrete panel joint profile also makes it difficult to attain continuous contact with the panel edge. Cruciform gaskets are produced in rolls, and are difficult to straighten out.

The cost of the jointing system depends on the quality of the materials used. For sealant joints, the cost is generally related to the volume of sealant, and is influenced by the expected range of joint sizes. For gaskets, the labour in cutting and welding the section and the correct selection of gasket size are of particular significance.

Removal of moisture from behind panels

No matter which type of joint is used, there is a general consensus of opinion by BRE and panel manufacturers that from time to time moisture will occur on the inner surface of panels as a result of condensation and/or rain penetration, and panels should be designed to include facilities for its removal by weepholes left in the moulding. Condensation is collected in a groove on top of the bottom horizontal ribs. Different weephole designs and condensation grooves are shown in Fig. 1.28. Weepholes should not be less than 13 mm internal diameter to prevent blocking, and they should project from the face of the building to prevent, as far as possible, any staining of the panel surface. In order to prevent such staining, it is sometimes possible for the weephole to be cast into the panel so that it drains moisture into the horizontal joint.

Panel fixings

Panels can be either top hung from the structure or supported from their base. Nibs projecting from the back of the panel transmit the load to the structure by means of a mortar bed. Panels can then be restrained either by dowel bars or by angle cleats, both of which must be fixed so as to permit vertical movements arising from the deformation of the structure or movement of the panels. Various combina-

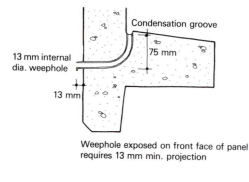

Fig. 1.28 Alternative positions of weepholes.

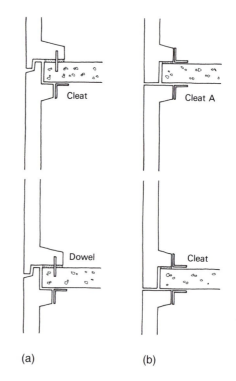

(a)   (b)

Fig. 1.29 Various combinations of dowel and cleat fixings: (a) cleat to dowel bottom; (b) cleats top and bottom.

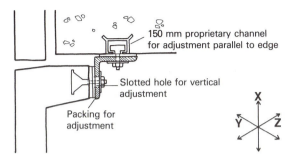

Fig. 1.31 Method of adjustment with cleat fixing offering movement in x, y and z axes.

tions of dowel and cleat fixings are shown in Fig. 1.29. Contractors often prefer cleat fixings at the top with dowel or cleat fixings at the bottom (types a and b) because this facilitates quick erection; however, building inspectors sometimes prefer panels to overhang the slab, as in theory should the fixing fail the panel would fall inwards under its own weight and wind loading.

Although the dimensional inaccuracies in manufacture of medium-sized precast concrete panels are not likely to be in excess of ±3 mm, the inaccuracies imposed during assembly because of deviations in the frame and erection deviations on these panels are likely to be much more than this, possibly ±25 mm. Thus tolerance must be allowed in the method of fixing and in the allowable clearance between the panels and the structure to take account of such inaccuracies of construction. Allowance must be made in the design of the fixings for thermal movement of the panel (Fig. 1.30). Avoid three fixings at different levels (Fig. 1.31). Two types of fixing are in common use in addition to the fixings for handling listed earlier. These are:

—   angle cleats;

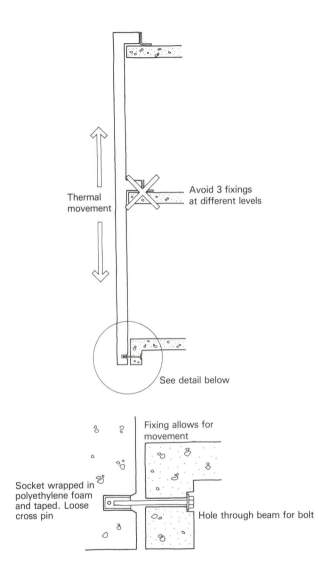

Fig. 1.30 Allowance in the design of fixings for thermal movement and inaccuracy.

Angle cleats

Although usually used for top restraint panels, angle cleats may also be employed at the base support position. There should be at least two cleats per panel, irrespective of panel size, and their size should be calculated by a structural engineer according to the loading for each job. They should be designed to give three-dimensional adjustments by the use of slotted holes and/or by packing pieces. Figure 1.31 shows a typical angle cleat system with packing allowance adjustment at right angles to the face of the building. Vertical adjustment is provided by the use of a slotted hole and low-friction washer, and horizontal adjustment is provided by means of a 150 mm length of proprietary channel cast into the floor slab. Care is needed in the accurate location of such channels during the casting of the slab, and reliable placing is more easily achieved when this channel is cast into the soffit of the slab (where it can be fastened to the shuttering), rather than in the top surface.

Bolts fixing the angle cleats are normally fixed to cast-in sockets or expanding sleeves. Cast-in sockets are used with precast concrete, as they can be accurately cast in place in the factory. However, with *in situ* concrete, their precise location cannot be guaranteed, and channels are used to allow adjustment. Where channels are not suitable, the structure is drilled to receive bolts with expanding sleeves, taking care to avoid reinforcement.

In all fixings relying on bolts or set screws, the designer must ensure that there is adequate space for tightening the bolt, or other device, in the completed assembly.

Dowel fixings

Dowel bar fixings are a common and simple method of locating and restraining the panel at its bottom

Fig. 1.32 Ribbed concrete panels.

support nibs. The main reason for their use is that they are considerably cheaper than non-ferrous angle cleats and can more easily accommodate dimensional inaccuracies in the structure. Usually, they are set in a 50 mm × 50 mm pocket in the *in situ* floor slab, a 50 mm diameter hole being provided in the panel to receive the dowel bar. The space around the dowel is grouted with either neat cement or an epoxy resin grout.

Where dowels are used in conjunction with panels supported at their head, some provision for vertical movement may be required. In this case, the bars can be bound with Sellotape to avoid adhesion of the grout. A resilient pad between the panel nibs allows movement and prevents grout loss.

Finishes

The range of finishes that can be produced on precast cladding can be summarized according to their method of production as:

- surfaces cast direct from the mould, e.g. smooth centre, board-marked concrete, grooved or serrated, including reconstructed stone finishes;
- finishes in which the cement surface is removed to expose the aggregate in the concrete;
- applied finishes, such as tiles, stone facings and bricks;
- surfaces textured by tamping or shaping.

The various methods to produce these finishes are dealt with by Gage (1974) in his guide to exposed concrete finishes. In addition, examples of various exposed aggregate finishes can be seen in Oram (1978). Most precast concrete cladding panels use such exposed aggregate finishes, and their colour and texture are largely affected by the type of aggregate used. The use of applied finishes affects the type of casting used (Fig. 1.10).

Many buildings incorporate natural stone-faced cladding fixed with dowels or retention angles, and it is clear from examples of failures seen recently that there is a need to detail the fixings of stone panels to avoid spalling of the stone facing. Manufacturers normally advise the minimum thickness of limestone as 60 mm and of granite as 50 mm. Fixing dowels must not penetrate the stone to more than two-thirds of its thickness.

The incorporation of stone into curtain walling has promoted an interest in lightweight stone cladding consisting of a thin layer of natural stone (granite, marble or limestone) bonded to a unidirectional glass filament and phenolic resin skin bonded either side of an aluminium honeycomb core. Panels can be typically produced to a maximum size of 2400 mm × 1200 mm, 25 mm thick. Typical weight is 25 kg/m^2 compared with 50 mm thick granite, which weighs 135 kg/m^2, and 60 mm thick limestone, 144 kg/m^2.

Weathering

The quantity of rainwater, the velocity and the angle at which it hits a building change for different positions in the building, and therefore one must expect unequal weathering of the parts. This is particularly true for precast concrete, for which water absorption can cause blotches or streaking on finished surfaces. Concrete finishes vary considerably in their ability to take up and release dirt under weathering conditions. They should, therefore, be chosen for so-called self-cleansing properties.

Some buildings have been designed to take advantage of the unequal weathering in the profile of the panel: for example, faceted panels (now removed) were used at the mathematics building at

Fig. 1.33 Precast concrete arches at Seville Expo 1992 by Peter Rice.

Liverpool University (architects: Westwood, Piet, Poll and Smart). Vertical ribs or striations also help the appearance of panels. Panels for Portsmouth Dockyard (architects: Arup Associates) were produced by Minsterstone, using concrete moulds and ribbed to control weathering marks (Fig. 1.32).

The imaginative use of precast concrete panels by Peter Rice was shown in the precast concrete arches at Seville Expo (Fig. 1.33).

References

BPCF (1973) *Precast Concrete Cladding Panels – Method of Attachment, Support and Joint Design*, British Precast Concrete Federation, London.

BRE (1967) *Joints between concrete wall panels: open drained joints*, BRE Digest 85, Building Research Establishment, Garston, August.

Brookes, A. and Yeomans, D. (1981) Precast Concrete Cladding (Art of Construction Series), *Architects' Journal*, **133** (25), 1217–1224.

Cement & Concrete Association (1977) *Guide to Precast Concrete Cladding*, Technical Report No 14, Concrete Society, London.

Dawson, S. (1995) *Cast in Stone*, Architectural Cladding Association, London.

Gage, M. (1974) *Finishes in Precast Concrete*, Architectural Press, London (also published in *Architects' Journal*, 26 March 1969).

Gilchrist Wilson, J. (1963) *Concrete Facing Slabs*, Cement and Concrete Association, London.

Hartland, R. A. (1975) *Design of Precast Concrete*, Surrey University Press.

Morris, A. E. J. (1966) *Precast Concrete Cladding*, Fountain Press, London.

Oram, J. (1978) *Precast Concrete Cladding*, Cement and Concrete Association, London.

PCI (1973) *Architectural Precast Concrete*, Pre-Stressed Concrete Institute, Chicago.

Property Services Agency Method of Building (1978) *Technical Guidance on Precast Concrete – Non-loadbearing Cladding*, MOB doc. 01.704, 2nd edn, PSA Library, London, December.

Glass-reinforced polyester

Introduction

Many different materials have been used to form composites within the field of reinforced plastics. The concept is to combine a strong tensile fibrous material, to give tensile strength, with a resinous binder to hold the material together and provide compressive strength. Thus GRP is a composite of durable resin with glass-fibre reinforcement. Its principal characteristics are as follows:

—   It has a high strength and low density, leading to lightweight products. Despite its high tensile strength, however, it has a low modulus of elasticity, and therefore high loads can be sustained only at the expense of large deflections.
—   Glass-reinforced polyester has good corrosion and weather resistance, making it suitable for long-term use in external conditions.
—   Its most useful characteristic is that, being a thermosetting material, it can be moulded without the use of pressure or high temperature. This characteristic makes the moulding of relatively short runs of large awkward shapes possible. It also gives GRP its versatility of appearance as, in theory, almost any colour or texture can be produced.

Glass-reinforced polyester is more expensive on a volume basis than most other building materials, and it is therefore essential to use it in thin sections to achieve cost comparability.

To understand how GRP behaves in use, it is first necessary to understand the process of manufacture. The **gel coat**, a layer of resin that forms the outer surface of the GRP, provides protection for a mixture of glass-fibre reinforcement and a polyester **lay-up** resin. Coloured pigments can be added either to the resin or to the gel coat, and, in addition, chemicals and fillers can be added to improve the fire retardancy of the composite.

The liquid resin is **polymerized** or cured into a hard solid by the addition of chemical catalysts, which are mixed into the resin shortly before the material is laid up – in the mould – with the glass fibre. Any of these factors can change for a particular application. Unlike profiled steel, aluminium, or even precast concrete, for which – within limits – the constituents remain constant, with GRP there are a number of variables that could affect the long-term durability of the material, unless it is designed with care. In most cases the laminate is laid up using hand rollers or spray techniques in contact moulds. Mechanical processes such as vacuum bags or press mouldings are only really applicable for long production runs.

GRP production

Thus the factors of GRP production to be discussed further are:

- the polyester resin;
- the glass-fibre reinforcement;
- fabrication – the mould;
- quality control and faults in curing.

Polyester resin

The resin is supplied as a viscous syrup, which, when chemically activated, sets to a hard solid, binding the glass fibre together. Pigments can be added to the resin to provide the required colour. Finely ground filler may also be added to increase the resin's viscosity or improve its fire performance. Ultraviolet stabilizers may be added to reduce discoloration of GRP when exposed to sunlight. These pigments, fillers and stabilizers, however, in turn may affect the properties of the resin. The liquid polyester resin is polymerized into its hard solid state by the addition of chemical catalysts, preferably under controlled heat conditions. (Polyester materials are thermosetting, which signifies that they cannot be turned back into liquid form, unlike thermoplastic materials, such as polyethylene.) The mixing of resin and catalyst takes place shortly before the material is required for fabrication. The hardening process is sometimes called **curing**, and the rate of cure is temperature dependent.

A vital part played in the manufacturing process is that of ensuring that the final product is fully cured, for it is only in this state that structural and dimensional stability are ensured. Excessive catalyst will cause the mixture to overheat, because the chemical reaction produced is exothermic, resulting in cracking and crazing, while inadequate catalyst will produce an inadequate state of curing. (Such typical faults are contained in Chapter 6 of Scott Bader Co. Ltd (1980); see Fig. 2.1.) Usually, after demoulding, the panels are placed in a curing box under controlled temperature and humidity conditions. The manufacturer can make special curing boxes for large panels, although space in the factory may not necessarily be available, and the optimum size of the available kilns should be checked in advance of the design.

Glass-fibre reinforcement

Molten glass can be drawn out into a filament of glass fibre, and in this form has an ultimate tensile strength per area 10 times that of steel. The existence of the material has been known since the Egyptian XVIIIth Dynasty, about 1500 BC (Fibreglass Ltd, 1977a). However, glass fibres of sufficient fineness and consistency for reinforced plastics were not commercially available until the 1930s.

Although several types of glass can be drawn into fibres, the standard fibre used for all resin systems is E glass, which is a high-quality electrical-grade glass fibre. This is bundled together to form strands, which in turn can be processed into various products.

Chopped strand mat

This is the most common form of general-purpose reinforcement, which is used mainly for the hand-laminating process.

Continuous strand mat

In continuous strand mat the strands are not chopped, but just allowed to swirl randomly. The product is used for press moulding and resin injection moulding.

Continuous rovings

These consist of long bundles of fibres, which are fed into a machine that chops and sprays them onto the moulding in conjunction with the resin. This **spray-up** technique is used very widely to reduce the labour content of normal hand lay-up moulding.

A continuous thread of glass

This can be wound round the component being impregnated with the resin as it proceeds. This filament winding process produces high-performance components such as pressure piping, but is limited in form, and is expensive to set up.

Other reinforcement materials have been developed that give improved properties, albeit at increased cost. These are **carbon fibre**, a crystalline fibre devel-

a

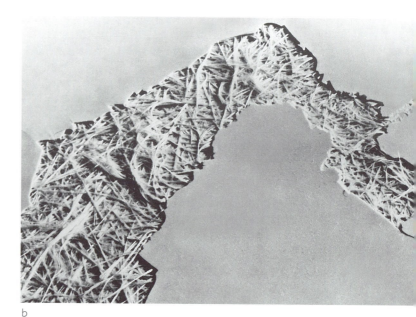

b

Fig. 2.1 Faults: (a) crazing of GRP surface; (b) internal dry patch.

oped by the Royal Aircraft Establishment in 1963, with a strength and modulus superior to that of glass fibre, and **aramid fibre**, a lightweight, low-modulus fibre developed by Du Pont Industrial Fibres, under the trademark of Kevlar.

Fabrication – the mould

The process of fabrication involves laying up successive layers of resin, into which glass-fibre reinforcement is embedded to follow a mould profile (Fig. 2.2). Reid and O'Brien (1973) have described the basic laying-up techniques. The open mould **contact process** uses either hand lay-up or spray-up application. There are, in addition, some other mechanized processes, such as **press moulding** (hot or cold), using matching moulds to press out panels so that both sides of the panel have moulded surfaces. The moulds for this process are expensive and are more difficult to adapt to accommodate variations in panel shape. Other processes use **resin-injected techniques**, in which the glass-fibre reinforcement is placed in a mould of the required shape and resin is forced under pressure, or a combination of pressure and vacuum, into the mould space.

Hand lay-up or contact process

The simplest and most common method of building up the reinforcement and resin is by the hand lay-up technique. First, the mould is waxed and polished using a non-silicone-based wax (Fig. 2.3). It is usually sufficient to do this once every three to five usages of the mould. A release agent, the most common type being polyvinyl alcohol (PVAL), is then applied over the entire surface of the mould and allowed to dry thoroughly. When the mould has been 'run in', it is possible to do away with this operation, except at the edges, relying only on the waxed surface for separation.

The durability of a moulding is mainly dependent on its surface. Moisture will attack the glass-

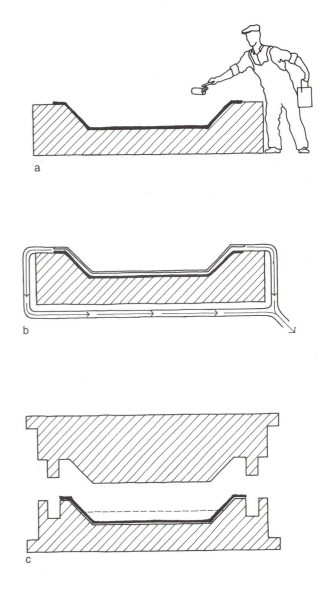

Fig. 2.2 Methods of GRP preparation: (a) contact moulding; (b) vacuum moulding: (c) press moulding.

fibre reinforcement so it is protected by a layer of resin known as the **gel coat**. This gel coat is applied to the mould by brush or roller at 450–600 g/m². Gel coat resins differ from lay-up resins in that they are thixotropic to avoid draining from a vertical surface, and they also gel with a tacky surface where exposed to air to facilitate a good bond to the rest of the laminate. The utmost care and skill are needed in this operation if an even coating is to be achieved without the entrainment of air bubbles or trapping of dirt. The thickness should be carefully controlled, for where the coating is in excess of 600 μm thick, crazing and cracking, coupled with reduced impact resistance in use, are likely to occur. Faults in the surface of the gel coat will result in water penetration and a subsequent breakdown of the glass-fibre reinforcement, leading to swelling and rupture of the laminate.

For a small moulding, mixing is done by the laminator using a volume-measuring device to measure in the catalyst. In the simplest case it is done by hand. Where larger volumes are required, measuring and mixing would be done by a machine in a separate area under the charge of a responsible person.

The lay-up of the glass-fibre reinforcement and resin can start as soon as the gel coat has hardened sufficiently not to come away on the finger when touched. The resin is mixed as before and a liberal coat is applied over the gel coat. The optimum quantity of lay-up resin can be calculated from the weight of glass reinforcement. For chopped strand mat the resin : glass ratio should be between 2.5 : 1 and 2 : 1 by weight. The first layer of reinforcement is pressed into the mould and consolidated with a brush or roller. The lay-up is consolidated with a roller, and subsequent layers of resin and glass mat are applied until the required thickness is built up. Figure 2.4 shows rolling out the lay-up to remove air bubbles.

Fig. 2.3 Mould waxing prior to moulding.

Fig. 2.4 Rolling out the lay-up to remove air bubbles.

Spray lay-up

An alternative method of building up the resin and reinforcement in the contact moulding procedure is by the simultaneous deposition of resin and chopped glass fibre by spray-moulding equipment. **Spray lay-up** considerably reduces the labour content of the process, although rolling out is still required to consolidate the laminate and ensure that the resin is mixed.

Machine moulding

There are several methods of producing GRP mouldings by more mechanized methods than the contact moulding technique described so far. These mechanized processes, such as **resin injection, vacuum forming** and **pultrusion** (only applicable to long continuous runs) are not normally relevant to cladding units. This is partly because of the limits of size possible with these processes, and partly because of the capital investment in the necessary machinery. Cladding panels are not often produced in long continuous runs, and because architects are normally designing a one-off panel system requiring only a few hundred panels, the capital outlay for relatively sophisticated machinery becomes inapplicable. One of the few exceptions to this would be the roof panels for Covent Garden Market, London, which were produced by Armshire Reinforced Plastics using resin injection and pressing techniques (Holloway, 1975, p. 69).

It is interesting to make a comparison with the boat-building industry, where this 'tooling up' process is done once and is paid for by the production of a large number of products. In cladding this would require a complete development programme every time a new contract was initiated. Glass-reinforced polyester being a complex design material leads to development time for this process to take place, whereas building components, such as cladding, are often subcontracted, there being a short time between the design and requirement of the product, putting the manufacturer under considerable pressure to met specific deadlines in relation to other design work construction processes. Hand lay-ups and spray techniques are slow; the production of one panel per day per mould is the norm, causing the manufacturer to use a number of moulds to meet the requirement. This in turn increases costs, coupled with the fact that a mould may only last 50–100 panels, after which it would have to be discarded.

The mould

Before an item can go into production, a considerable amount of work has to be done to prepare the mould required for its manufacture. The quality of the mould will ultimately dictate the quality of the finished product. For most projects where a number of panels are required, the moulds are formed of GRP. Master patterns can be made in materials such as timber, steel or plaster, from which this GRP mould is taken. A GRP laminate during curing may shrink by 0.1–0.4% (linearly), and as there are two moulding processes between the pattern and the finished product, the net shrinkage may be as much as 0.8% (one manufacturer gave as an example a 9 m long panel being over-sized by 1.2 mm to allow for shrinkage). The manufacturer gradually knows from experience how much to allow for shrinkage, depending upon the shape of the unit, the resin and the temperature change expected. Tooling is one of the highest costs in GRP manufacture. Moulders and finishers are considered to be skilled labour, and most of the larger manufacturers have introduced training schemes for apprentices to this trade.

Because of the bespoke nature of the industry and the number of panels involved for each job, the manufacturers cannot afford too many prototypes before a satisfactory target dimension is achieved. A large number of panels will have to be produced for a number of moulds, not all necessarily to the same master pattern. This is a factor affecting manufacturing deviations of panel size (tolerances).

Another difficulty of manufacture is that some of the stresses set up in the matrix are inherent, produced by the differential shrinkage between fibre and resin when the GRP composite is cooled to room temperature during fabrication, as a result of differing coefficients of thermal expansion ($70{-}100 \times 10^{-6}\,°C$ for resin versus $5.0 \times 10^{-6}\,°C$ for glass). Resin additives can alleviate these effects by reducing shrinkage.

Although it is clearly desirable to design for simple moulds, it is possible to develop **split moulds** with movable sections to achieve return angles. A flash line is then seen on the face of the panel at the junction of the two sections of the mould. It is possible to buff this out in finishing operations, or render it less obvious by designing the 'split' to coincide with a change of profile. It is vital that reasonable access be given to the fabricator in order to lay up evenly all sections of the mould and to facilitate consolidation of the material by means of a hand roller to expel any air bubbles that may be entrained in the laminate. Too large a mould, or one of a complicated shape, means that the fabricator cannot get to all the areas in order to lay up an even coating of glass fibre and resin, while at the same time ensuring good compaction and ease of rolling out. The ideal panel width is one for which the operator can reach all parts of the mould easily, say 2 m wide. The domed panels at Castle Park, Nottingham (architects: Nicholas Grimshaw Partnership) were manufactured as one-piece units using a tilting mould allowing access to all areas for the fabricator. These tilting moulds are similar to those used in boat production (Fig. 2.5).

Fig. 2.5 Tilting moulds being used for production.

Quality control and faults in curing

Because the GRP panel industry has a high labour content, the designer/purchaser is totally dependent upon the quality of the labour force employed and the conditions under which they work in the factory. Environmental control on the shopfloor is very important in terms of evenness in temperature and constant relative humidity if the final product is going to be lasting and of good quality. For an illustration of a typical production process, see Fig. 2.6.

Although in its simplest form the laying up of glass fibre in layers looks easy, the process leading to the successful application in large wall elements is much more complicated. There is the initial difficulty of choosing a resin to make a laminate by reference to the resin properties alone. The properties and performance required of the whole matrix must be considered for different resins, and their additives will perform different functions with regard to weathering, flame retardance and colour stability. Depending upon choice, these various constituents may be used in different proportions to each other, and the right control of temperature and humidity limits is essential. The temperature in the workshop should be controlled between 18°C and 25°C, and ideally should be maintained overnight. The workshop should not be damp, as this causes the glass reinforcement to soak up water, and could lead to delamination of the finished article and a breaking up of the resin/glass-fibre matrix. Cleanliness is of importance, as any contamination in the lay-up will degrade appearance and strength, while good ventilation is also a necessity in order to control styrene content in the atmosphere.

Cutting catalyst levels and reducing workshop

Fig. 2.6 Typical GRP production with large curing box at the rear of the factory.

temperatures will produce inferior laminates, which perform badly. Blemishes can include gel-coat wrinkling, surface pinholing, poor adhesion of the gel coat and resin, spotting of the gel-coat surface, striation in pigment flotation, pattern of fibres visible through a gel coat, patches of pale colour or 'fish eyes', blisters, crazing of surface of resin, and star mat and leaching after leaving glass fibre exposed to moisture.

As the performance and durability of the GRP product depend mainly on the cure of the polyester resin, it is essential that there should be some means of establishing whether or not the laminate is suspect. Such a method is recommended in Appendix A of BS 4549, Part 1: 1970 *Guide to quality control requirements for reinforced plastic mouldings*, the 'Barcol test', which is a form of the impact test.

The weight of the laminate measured against that of the requirements laid down in the specification will give a check as to whether a layer of reinforcement has been omitted, while the Barcol test for hardness, although not giving an absolute measurement of the cure, will differentiate between a really bad laminate and a reasonable one with a little more accuracy than is possible by casual observation. The laminate should have a hardness of around 35 within a few days. Post-curing for 16 hours at 40°C can improve this to around 40 with decreased water absorption and little effect on the other mechanical properties. Test laminates can be used to check the strength of a specified lay-up, although these may not necessarily be representative of the overall quality achieved in the product.

The heat distortion point for GRP is particularly important for cladding applications where high external temperatures are expected: for example, the use of dark-coloured panels in south-facing elevations. For such applications, resins with higher heat distortion points must be used, while it is vital that test and post-curing are carried out at or above temperatures that the panel may sustain in use. Any creep in the material that can be anticipated can be taken into account in the design by adding stiffeners to the panel.

To achieve a quality product, therefore, it is necessary for the panel to be manufactured in the right conditions, by experienced workers, in the correct proportion, using the right techniques. Ignorance of these controls may lead to what appears to be a satisfactory product on the shopfloor, but one that is unlikely to perform satisfactorily throughout its expected design life. All this leads to a situation where great care has to be taken in quality control during production. It is not outside the designer's field to be able to set out these conditions in the specification, and it is essential to request record sheets from the manufacturer for each unit provided. Manufacturers should therefore be asked whether they:

—   keep a record sheet for each unit manufactured, containing a unique reference number, date of casting, mix details, tests carried out, etc.;
—   check weighing of each unit after curing;
—   have an established procedure for dealing with minor blemishes and defects discovered in the units at various stages.

Some specifiers have found it necessary to have direct quality control over all the units during manufacture. The specification for the works and materials at Mondial House, London, for example, includes a clause that 'each panel will be inspected dimensionally, and for gel surface defects and signs of poor laminating, by the consultants and marked if approved'. The GRP panels for the Herman Miller factory at Bath were also inspected individually by the architects, Farrell and Grimshaw, in the factory. Although this may still be necessary for prestigious jobs, most reputable manufacturers will now have the correct quality control procedures. Indeed, it could be said that architects' standards for cladding are higher than can be reasonably expected, and it is interesting to reflect that GRP-coffered slab formers are often acceptable with lower standards of workmanship.

GRP cladding in use

The first applications of GRP in the building industry were in the mid 1950s, when there was intense design activity in the material. In 1956 the Monsanto 'House of the Future' was exhibited at Disneyland, making revolutionary use of structural GRP. By 1961 the technology had been advanced to the point where GRP foam sandwich buildings had been erected as relay rooms for British Railways, and the system extended to produce a research laboratory in the Antarctic. In 1966 pressed GRP panels with a concrete backing were produced by the Indulex Engineering Company, used at a multi-storey block of flats in Paddington, London, and known as the SFI System (Building Research Association of New Zealand, 1981). With this rapid advance in the application of the material, it is not surprising that many people expected a breakthrough in the advance of GRP structures leading to the widespread use of the material in building. This breakthrough has never really come about. Glass-reinforced polyester has, however, established itself in some less wide-ranging areas of building construction, the premier one being the manufacture of cladding panels.

The simplicity of the manufacturing process allowed many small fabricators to set up without the need for large capital expenditure. There are, however, only a handful who specialize in cladding and have had experience of large contracts. A designer wishing to use GRP as a cladding material, even now, 40 years after it was first used, is liable to face some difficulties. R. D. Gay (1965) at the Conference on Plastics in Building Structures stated:

> The data on properties of these materials do not exist in the form required – the plastics industry has not yet learned to present them in that way; some data are not yet available because the professions have not made known what they require and how. There are no codes of practice, and no textbooks are available for the design of building structures.

Thus the designer was dependent on information from the manufacturer, such as Fibreglass Ltd (1977b, 1977c).

Standardization of components

Because of its mouldability, GRP is often marketed offering a variety of shapes and sizes, and many manufacturers' catalogues stress its versatility of shape. Even so, economy of production can only be really achieved with standardized identical units.

Manufacturers' moulds are high-cost items, and repetitive identical units are desirable for maximum economy, although this similarity need not extend to uniformity of colour.

Specials or non-standard units increase costs and involve the structural engineer in numerous adjustments in the design of the fixings. Curved or shaped panels need special moulds.

If special units are to be incorporated it is an advantage if they are smaller than the standard-sized panel used in the majority of the scheme, for it is much easier to adapt the original mould than to make a new one for four or five specials. Gillingham Marina is a good example of the use of adaptable moulds using the same basic shape with filler pieces for door and window panels (Brookes and Ward, 1981, p. 1137).

Strangely, although we tend to associate the boat-building industry with one-off large boat designs, the reason why GRP is widely used for boats is that the production of large numbers of identical products pays for the initial tooling up and capital expenditure in such items as rotating moulds.

Fire resistance

In the UK a Class 0 resistant laminate to BS 476 is required for claddings on buildings above 15 m high, or Class 2 or 3, within 1 m of the boundary. In order to provide this degree of fire resistance, it has been usual to improve the fire retardancy of polyester resins by:

- the addition of fillers;
- the use of additives, such as antimony oxide plus chlorinated paraffin, which can be mixed up with the resin;
- building in certain groups in the chemical structure of the resin, for example dibromoneopentyl glycol, hexachloro-endomethylene, tetrachlorophthalic acid, chlorostyrene.

It has been found, however, that the weathering qualities of the laminate produced in these ways are reduced in positions exposed to ultraviolet rays, and even white will yellow with age.

An additional way is to coat the internal surface of the GRP structure with an intumescent coating. Intumescent polyesters are now available, which contain compounds designed to give a carbonaceous foam on application of a flame. However, all methods used so far in trying to improve the fire retardancy of polyester resins have considerably lowered

Fig. 2.7 Mondial House, London (architects: Hubbard Ford & Partners).

the GRP's resistance to breakdown (loss of gloss, colour change) when exposed to the outdoor environment. Tests have shown that on one common type of fire-retardant GRP sheet, using tetra-chlorophthalic acid polyester as an inhibitor, the surface deterioration was 2.5–3.0 times faster than that of sheets based on general-purpose/conventional polyester resins.

Another solution to the problem of providing the required fire rating has been to apply a two-pack polyurethane surface coating in order to protect the laminate from the effects of ultraviolet light: for example, An-o-clad by Anmac Ltd. This uses a modified gel-coat system, which in itself adds to the fire characteristics of the panel and is then coated with the two-pack polyurethane to give good weatherability. This system, when tested to BS 476 Part 7 for a Class I test, had 'nil' spread of flame on the test samples. Good resistance to the breakdown of the gel coat is also achieved by coating GRP panels with a lacquer based on an ultraviolet-stabilized acrylic resin.

A more usual solution is either to position the building away from the boundary or to ask for a relaxation to the Class 0 fire requirement. In this case a general-purpose isophthalic gel coat can be used, which itself has no fire-retardant characteristics, but which protects the laminating resin containing the fire-retardant additive from ultraviolet light. But, of course, it does not get a Class 0 fire rating. When applying for such a waiver it may be necessary for tests to be carried out that stimulate in-service conditions on full panels, including the appropriate jointing technique used. The configuration and design of the joints must significantly affect the performance of the panels during a fire. The panels for Mondial House (Fig. 2.7), designed by Peter Hodge Associates, and manufactured by Anmac Ltd and Brensal Plastics Ltd, were tested by Yarsley Laboratories. Two sets of fire tests were performed, the first on tested coupons in accordance with BS 476, the second on two complete panels with a joint, set up in the attitude to be used in service. A large gas flame with heat output of 190 W/min was set up beneath the bottom of the panels. The results of the test showed that there was no uncontrolled spread of flame over the surface, and even after an hour's exposure the panel still retained its form.

Incidentally, this project is probably the largest structure erected using GRP cladding in the UK, and the inclusion of mini-rib finish to these panels has resulted in their still maintaining their appearance almost 20 years since installation.

Thus the two main problems associated with GRP, that of weathering (especially as a result of ultraviolet degradation) and fire resistance, tend to work against each other. The addition of fillers and pigments to reach some sort of fire resistance acceptability through tests laid down in the Building Regulations tends to weaken the material's capacity to resist weathering, and a darkening of the surface pigments may take place.

Weathering

The selection of colour can significantly affect the overall weatherability of the panels. In general, the stronger colours, such as oranges and reds, have a tendency to fade under the effect of ultraviolet light; the ultraviolet light will cause the surface of the material to chalk. Architects often specify these colours in ignorance of the problems associated with some pigments, and all too often the manufacturers will supply the colours as requested. The current fashion for oranges, browns and reds has exaggerated this difficulty, which is not confined to GRP claddings.

In general, colouring of the GRP panels is best done by pigment in the resin or gel coat, and not as an applied finish. However, Blaga (1978) claims that good resistance to the effects of moisture- and/or temperature-induced stress fatigue is achieved by coating the GRP sheets with a lacquer based on ultraviolet-stabilized acrylic resin:

> The acrylic acting protects the glass-resin interface against the effects of stress fatigue and the underlying matrix against the action of UV light. This type of coating may be particularly useful for fire-resistant GRP sheets, which are especially susceptible to breakdown in outdoor exposure. Similarly, GRP sheets protected with a UV-stabilized (in-plant laminated) PVF surfacing film (0.025 mm thick) have remarkable resistance to the effect of weathering.

The difficulty may be to achieve a permanent bond between the laminate and this polyvinyl fluoride film (Tedlar).

Fig. 2.8 Blue GRP panels with red fascias used at the Water Research Centre, Swindon.

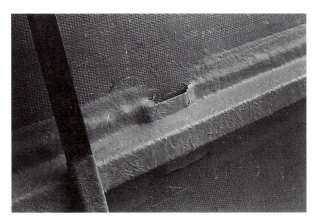

Fig. 2.9 Ventilated top-hat stiffener to prevent distortion during manufacture.

No completely satisfactory method of assessing the weathering resistance of plastics materials in service by laboratory simulation has yet been found. Weatherometer testing and xenon arc testing are popular methods, but these can, at most, give only an identification of performance in use. After 1000 hours' exposure to the xenon test, any change of colour should be moderate and uniform.

Blue GRP panels with red fascias were used at the Water Research Centre, Swindon. They have suffered from some colour fading (Figs 2.8).

Colour fastness tends to be uniform within any one batch of panels, but can vary from batch to batch. One method of anticipating differences in colour fastness between panels is to use a striped effect, as at the Olivetti factory, Haslemere (architect: James Stirling) (Fig. 2.10). The colour of the outer skin can also increase any possibility of delamination of sandwich panels due to temperature build-up on the surface. The darker the colour and the higher the temperature, the greater the risk of delamination. Interior use of GRP is usually successful.

In theory, minor blemishes in GRP can be made good on site, provided there are correct weather conditions, and a highly skilled labour force is available. In practice, such conditions hardly ever exist, and, as yet, methods of curing on site are not available. Thus normally the panels are returned to the factory for repair. To prevent accidental damage on site, it is important to protect the panels during assembly. Panels for the Herman Miller factory, for example, were protected with a plastic coating while being installed (Fig. 2.11).

Surface scratching, which can be caused by something as simple as a window cleaner's ladder that has no padded protection, produces unsightly defects. The client should be warned that if weather is allowed to get to the back of a panel, the uncoated side will deteriorate. Where panels such as balustrades are exposed to the weather on both sides it is necessary to gel coat both inner and outer surfaces. Condensation on the back face of a panel that has no gel-coat protection on its inner skin can also lead to premature breakdown of the laminate if the glass fibres are exposed at the surface.

Surface finish

Large shiny surfaces in GRP will show warping when used extensively over large, flat elevations. Panels up to 1 m wide with a high gloss can be accommodated, but over that width, surface ripple may become apparent. This is not only a problem of GRP – even plate glass and aluminium sheeting suffer in this respect. For this reason, some surface treatment may be appropriate, such as a matt-textured finish. Within reason, the coarser the texture the more surface deflection it will accommodate. However, if the texture becomes too coarse, it can slow down the rate of lamination, increasing the cost of production. Probably the optimum finish is a riven slate texture created in the master pattern mould, which has all the advantage of accommodating surface deflection, while being economical to laminate. However, riven slate has the disadvantage that it is limited in size and therefore has to be panelled, though this does not necessarily create difficulties if designed with care.

Vinyl cloth is very good for producing a light striated panel. For example, panels for a store in Nottingham, shown under construction in Fig. 2.12,

Fig. 2.10 Olivetti Training Centre at Haslemere (architect: James Stirling).

Fig. 2.11 Panels at Herman Miller factory, Bath (architects: Farrell and Grimshaw).

were produced with a matt surface after laying vinyl wallpaper onto the mould from which the production mould was manufactured. However, against this, vinyl cloth is available only in set widths, with resulting difficulties in hiding the joints. Random spray-on textures have advantages when compound curves are a feature of the design.

It is not uncommon, because of the ease of moulding GRP panels, for them to be used in conjunction with other materials for solving special corner or flashing details. For example, at the factory at Winwick Quay, Warrington (architects: Nicholas Grimshaw Partnership) (Fig. 2.13), GRP corner panels are painted to match the silver-grey Alucobond aluminium sandwich panels. This mixing of materials can lead to problems of colour matching and difference in rates of colour change.

Panel stiffening

Glass-reinforced polyester has a high tensile strength but low modulus of elasticity. Although it can accept

Fig. 2.12 Nottingham Co-op under construction.

Fig. 2.13 Corner panels at Winwick Quay (architects: Nicholas Grimshaw Partnership).

quite high loads, this is done only at the expense of great deformation or deflection. High deflections are undesirable as they can result in gel-coat cracking. Because of the cost of the material, thickening of the laminate overall would be too expensive. Four basic ways of stiffening panels in common use are shown in Fig. 2.14. These are:

— shaped profiles;
— ribbed construction;
— sandwich construction with foamed core;

— sandwich construction with sheet core.

Shaped profiles

Panels can be designed for stiffness in a geometric form. Even for a nominally flat panel, a shallow profile, pyramid, dome or dish can make a considerable improvement to its stiffness. In some cases it may be possible to design the panels so that the form for stiffening also acts structurally. For example, the spandrel panels at the American Express European Headquarters building at Brighton (architects: Gollins Melvin Ward Partnership), which are 7.2 m × 1.4 m × 0.8 m Class II GRP channel sections, not only form the cladding but also act as structural elements supporting the glazing above (Fig. 2.15)

Ribbed construction

Single-skin construction can be stiffened by a system of ribs on the back of the panel, such as those at Mondial House, London (Fig. 2.16). Ribs are normally made from GRP, laminated over a rib former in a mould, but they can also be formed by incorporating another material of appropriate shape and stiffness into the panel. Polyurethane foam or cardboard tubes can be used as rib formers. Where timber or metal sections are laminated into, or over-laminated onto, the back of the GRP skins, these materials have different coefficients of thermal expansion from that of the GRP, and it may be necessary to ensure a mechanical key grip rather than rely upon adhesion. Aluminium sections are particularly useful, because they have similar properties to GRP with regard to thermal expansion.

Rib patterning/shadowing on the face of the panel has also been known to occur, and some manufacturers have found that to overcome this the top-hat section or rib should be vented by cutting during the fabrication process (Fig. 2.9). This results in an even balance of temperature over the total face area of the panel when heat build-up occurs, either during curing or on site due to direct sunlight.

Sandwich construction

As an alternative to using shaped profiles or ribbed construction, it is possible to stiffen the panel using sandwich construction techniques. The advantages here are that the insulation is integral within the panel, cutting down on the number of site processes involved, thereby saving time, and the whole skin is manufactured

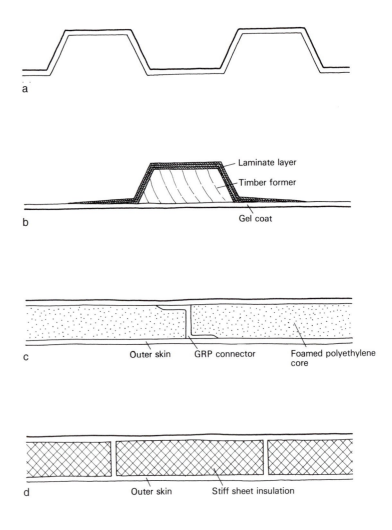

Fig. 2.14 Methods of stiffening GRP panels: (a) shaped profile; (b) ribbed construction; (c) sandwich construction using GRP connector and foamed insulation core; (d) sandwich construction – stiff insulation sheet laid into lamination.

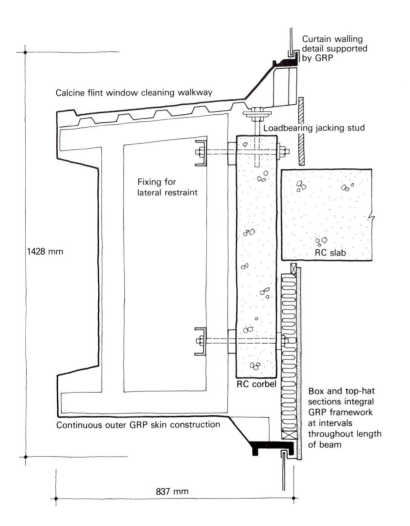

Curtain walling
detail supported
by GRP

Calcine flint window cleaning walkway

Loadbearing jacking stud

Fixing for
lateral restraint

RC slab

1428 mm

RC corbel

Continuous outer GRP skin construction

Box and top-hat
sections integral
GRP framework
at intervals
throughout length
of beam

837 mm

Fig. 2.15 Section through GRP panels at American Express building, Brighton (architects: Gollins Melvin Ward Partnership).

to the same tolerances and quality control within the factory.

In sandwich construction two skins of GRP are separated by an insulating core. The edge of the panels is usually formed by bringing the two laminates together. In order to ensure maximum structural connection between skins, it is customary to use GRP connectors at intervals when using foamed polyurethane. Problems can occur because of the differential expansion and contraction rates of the skin and the core. With poor bonding of core to face, surface blistering may occur.

Panels at the Herman Miller factory (Fig. 2.18) were produced by two separate sandwich skins, the function of the core being to keep the two skins a constant distance apart during deflection and to keep them rigidly connected so that they act as a composite element.

Jointing

Most problems of jointing GRP cladding panels occur at the external panel-to-panel joint, particularly at the crossover situation. These external joints and their jointing materials must be able to accommodate the thermal movements and deflection movements of the mouldings under maximum dead and live load conditions, as well as allowing for manufacturing tolerances and errors in erection.

Three types of joints are commonly used:

- mastic sealant joints;
- gasket joints;
- open-drained joints.

Mastic sealant joints

The performance of this type of joint depends on the

skill of the site applicator. There have been a number of examples of sealant failures with GRP panels. For example, the *Architects' Journal* (Reid and O'Brien, 1973) reported on two projects, *HMS Sealand* and British Gas Corporation, Solihull, where joints between panels showed unsightly mastic failure. This type of failure is often due to insufficient account being taken of the expected thermal and moisture movement at the design stage, and in some cases is caused by failure to remove all traces of releasing agent at the panel edge before sealant is applied. Recent developments in silicone rubbers have improved the performance of sealants because of their much greater movement accommodation and lower stress at the bond face.

Gasket joints

This type of joint normally incorporates a neoprene-extruded section; because they are factory produced, they are not so dependent on the site operative for their successful application. As an alternative to neoprene, ethylene propylene diamine monomer (EPDM) has better inherent resistance to oxidation attack and subsequent ageing. However, its drawback is poor resistance to attack from lubricating oils and various solvents. EPDM's ability to recover from compression is also less than that of neoprene. Although it is possible, according to their formulation, to obtain rubbers with good or bad tear resistance in both neoprene and EPDM, generally speaking EPDM has less resistance to tearing than neoprene, and thus is less easy to handle on site.

Site bonding of neoprene sections is now quite common for crossover joints. For example, the neoprene gasket joint used at the Herman Miller factory (Figs 2.19 and 2.20) is a simple glazing technique for both vertical and horizontal joints. A top-hat section is screwed into an aluminium carrier system, which

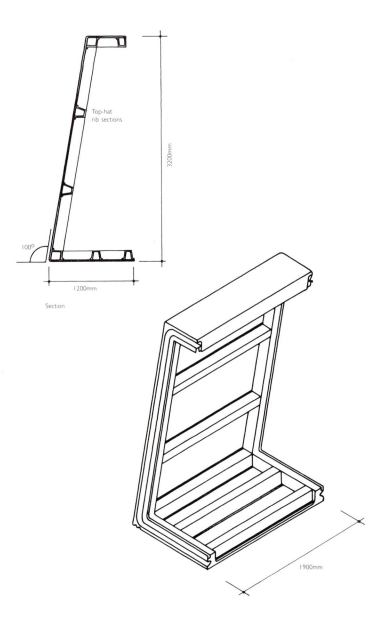

Fig. 2.16 Stiffening of GRP panels at Mondial House using GRP top hat and box sections (architects: Hubbard Ford & Partners).

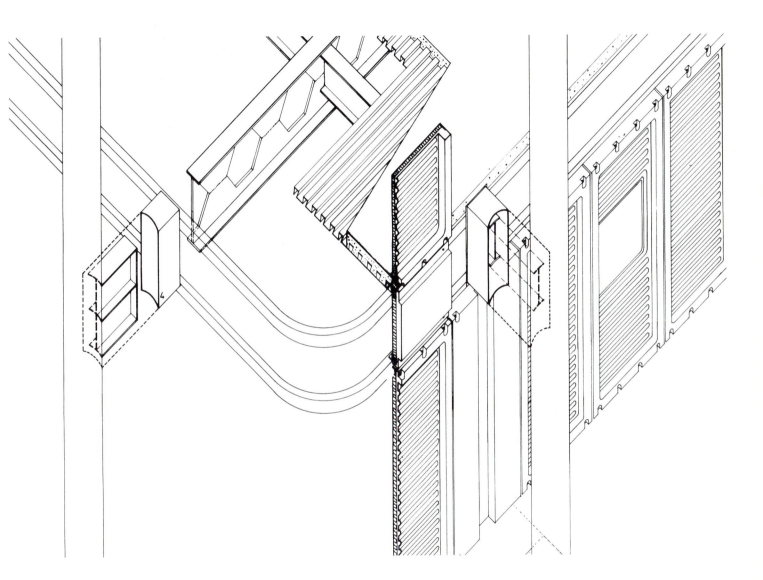

Fig. 2.17 Detail of GRP panels used at the Water Research Centre.

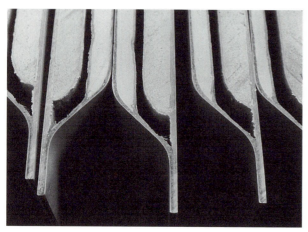

Fig. 2.18 Sandwich panels as used at the Herman Miller factory.

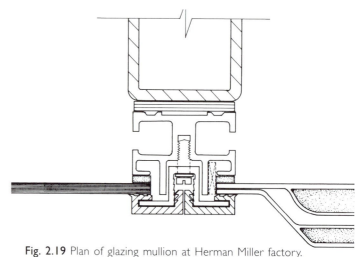

Fig. 2.19 Plan of glazing mullion at Herman Miller factory.

in turn is supported by the main framing. A continuous gasket is then pushed into this top-hat section. At parapet level the neoprene vertical joint changes to a narrow mastic sealant, because of difficulties in carrying the top-hat section over the curved jointing profile.

Neoprene gaskets work best when they are compressed within the joint, normally on the back side of the panel edge profile. A simple compressible gasket using timber edging pieces with GRP panels was developed for Teesside Polytechnic (architects: Basil Spence & Partners) (Fig. 2.21), for use with panels 1 m × 1 m. A more complicated gasket joint was developed for Mondial House (Hodge, 1968) (Fig. 2.22), which uses a combination of a neoprene baffle, a PVC back channel and a strip sealant under compression from a back plate. The joint was tested successfully by Yarsley Laboratories to BS 4315, simulating 18.75 cm of rain per hour at a wind speed of 56–64 km/h. This very sophisticated joint combines the principles of an open-drained joint with that of a labyrinth joint. As a result of this experience at Mondial House, Anmac Ltd developed its own 'patented' two-stage mechanical joint called LSB. This had the advantage that the jointing product is under compression and hidden from ultraviolet light.

Open-drained joints

This type of joint (see Fig. 1.23 for an example in concrete cladding) is not in widespread use with GRP panels. This may be because of the difficulties that can be experienced in casting the necessary depth of baffle groove. Other problems have been experienced in fixing the baffles at the top of the panel to prevent them from sliding down the groove. Open-drained joints at HMS Raleigh, Plymouth (Fig. 2.24), incorporated a bridging plate at the top of the joint in an attempt to stop the baffle from slipping. Specifications for the use of neoprene baffles should be in accordance with BS 4255 Part 1 : 1967 *Preformed rubber gaskets for weather exclusion from buildings*.

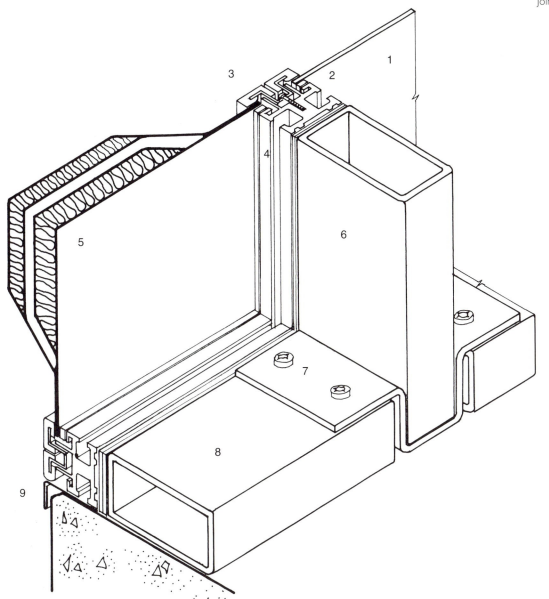

Fig. 2.20 Neoprene jointing gaskets used at the Herman Miller factory, Bath: (1) 6 mm surface-modified solar control glass: (2) resilient packing strip; (3) continuous neoprene gasket fitted to U-shaped aluminium beading screwed back to carrier; (4) extruded aluminium carrier screwed back to steel hollow section; (5) GRP sandwich panel, overall thickness 75 mm, outer insulation 19 mm polyurethane foam, inner insulation 25 mm polyurethane foam; (6) 127 mm × 63.5 mm hollow section steel subframe mullion; (7) 6 mm mild steel assembly shoe bolted to concrete slab; (8) 127 mm × 63.5 mm hollow section steel horizontal rail; (9) pressed aluminium sill fixed back behind carrier.

Fig. 2.21 Joints between panels at Teesside Polytechnic (architects: Basil Spence & Partners).

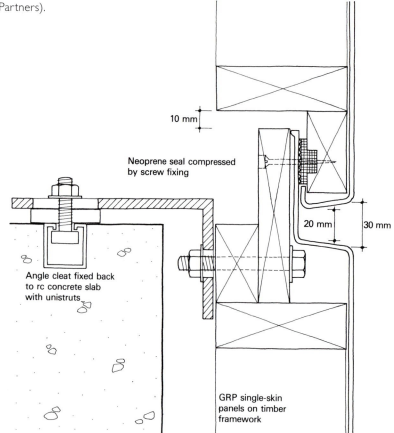

Thermal expansion

Glass-reinforced polyester has a lower coefficient of thermal expansion than those of other plastics, but higher than those of steel, glass or concrete, and similar to that of aluminium and wood. The coefficient of expansion is linked to the amount of glass-fibre con-

tent in the laminate: the higher the glass-fibre content, the lower is the coefficient of expansion. The expansion rate for a chopped strand mat laminate is higher than that of a combination of chopped strand mat and woven rovings.

In calculating thermal movements the designer needs to assume a realistic figure for the tempera-

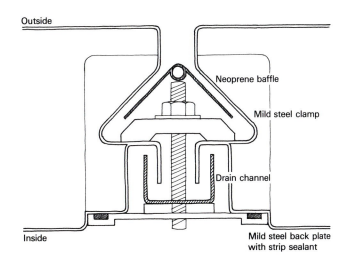

Outside

Neoprene baffle

Mild steel clamp

Drain channel

Inside

Mild steel back plate
with strip sealant

Fig. 2.22 Vertical joint at Mondial House.

ture gradient set up within the cross-section of the panel. This will depend upon factors such as orientation, colour of cladding, any insulation that may be behind it (sandwich panel), and its fixing and jointing aspects.

It is important to take account of thermal expansion in the design of fixings at the interface of GRP panels and some other finish material or component within the structure.

Fixings

It is obviously not possible to fit the panels on site to an absolutely true and level structure. Tolerances on the base structure must be notified to the designer of the GRP panel system, and reference should be made to BS 5606, which indicates the accuracy of assembly that may be expected on site for given components and construction.

One of the difficulties of fixing any single-skin panel back to the supporting structure is the problem of restraining the fixing device within the thickness of the panel. Several methods have been tried, including fixing plates moulded into the backs of the panels incorporating bolt fixings. Most uses, however, depend upon a system of clamping the panel back to the structure, usually at the joint interface. The American Express building in Brighton uses this method (Anon, 1977). Panels fixed at Mondial House incorporated a non-ferrous threaded fixing plate device hooked back onto the perimeter I-beam. The length of fixing involved resulted in this being an expensive way of achieving the necessary adjustments (Fig. 2.25).

Generally speaking, panels should be fixed rigidly at one point, with all other fixings being designed to accommodate the movement likely to occur. The rigid fixing must in itself be able to be adjusted to accom-

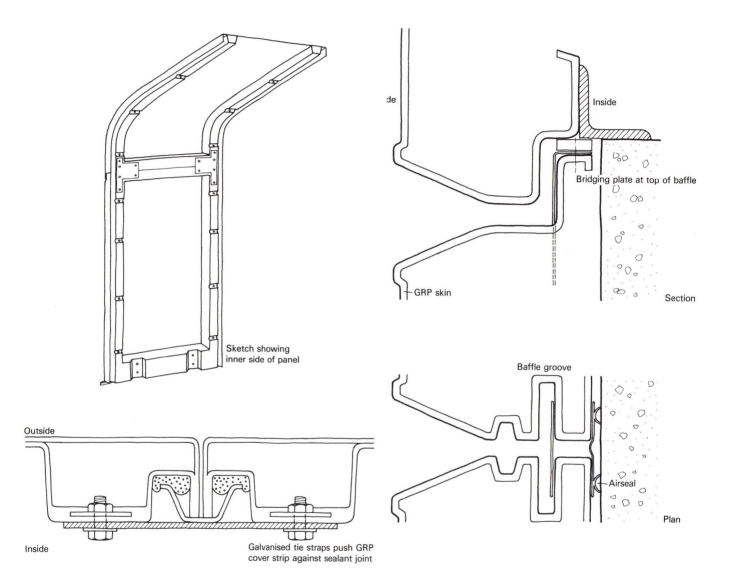

Sketch showing
inner side of panel

Outside

Inside

Galvanised tie straps push GRP
cover strip against sealant joint

de   Inside

Bridging plate at top of baffle

GRP skin   Section

Baffle groove

Airseal

Plan

Fig. 2.23 Typical back sealed joints between GRP units.

Fig. 2.24 Open-drained joint at HMS Raleigh (architects: PSA).

modate the manufacturing and building tolerances (BRE Digest 223 *Wall Cladding: designing to minimize effects due to inaccuracies and movement*). Often designers allow for mild steel stiffeners within the flanges of GRP. If these are subsequently site drilled for bolt fixings and not treated or sealed, moisture penetration will lead to rusting and delamination of the flanges.

The designer may need to consider fixings for handling; large panels are often difficult to handle on site because of high wind speeds coupled with their own light weight, and the size and number of fixings for a large panel need careful consideration. Although GRP as a material is relatively tough, surface protection during transport and erection on site to avoid surface scratching may be recommended (Fig. 2.26).

Conclusion

It can be seen from the foregoing sections that the manufacture of successful GRP moulding is far from the simple process that it may appear at first sight.

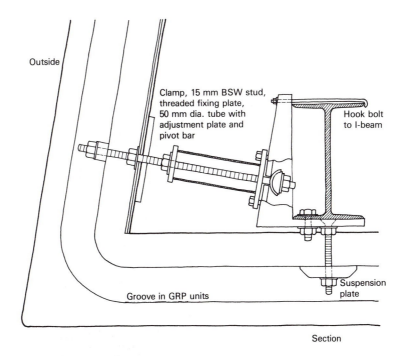

Fig. 2.25 Fixing to I-beam at Mondial House (architects: Hubbard Ford & Partners).

Although, in its simplest form, laying up layers of glass fibre is relatively easy, the process required to design and fabricate a product to satisfy its function for many years in a hostile environment is much more complicated. There are many types of resin and reinforcement, which can be modified by additives and fillers. The products have to be fabricated in the correct proportions by the right techniques and under the correct conditions to obtain a quality product.

Great care has to be taken in designing the correct stiffening of the panel using ribbed or sandwich construction, although more problems can be associated with the latter. Jointing and fixings must be carefully considered to take account of any thermal movement and inaccuracies (spacing, plumb and alignment) of the structural supports, and detailed specifications of the required standards of manufacture, assembly and repair are essential.

Finally, specification of detailing, fixing and jointing is just as important as requirements for resins, pigment additives and types of glass fibre to be used. Many problems have in the past been attributed to the properties of GRP, when in essence the problem may lie elsewhere. As with all panel systems, the component will only perform as well as its jointing and fixing allow it to.

References

Anon (1977) GRP cladding panels at American Express headquarters, Brighton. *Building Specification*, November.

Blaga, A. (1978) GRP composite materials in construction. *Industrialization Forum*, **9** (1).

Brookes, A. J. and Ward (1981) The art of construction – GRP claddings. *Architects' Journal*, 10 June; 17 June.

Building Research Association of New Zealand (1981) *Glass fibre reinforced polyester cladding panels. (1) Materials and manufacture; (2) Design, durability and maintenance,*

Fig. 2.26 Protection of panels using plastic coating during installation.

Building Information Bulletins 228 and 229, September, Building Research Association of New Zealand, Wellington.

Fibreglass Ltd (1977a) *Properties of glass fibres*, Information Sheet FIS 1050, February.

Fibreglass Ltd (1977b) *Materials for contract moulding*, Information Sheet FIS 1030, February.

Fibreglass Ltd (1977c) *Properties of fibreglass thermoset composites*, Information Sheet FIS 1052, February.

Gay, R. D. (1965) Conference on Plastics in Building Structures, The Plastics Institute, London.

Hodge, P. (1968) *Glass Reinforced Resin for Structure*, Peter Hodge and Associates, London.

Holloway, L. (1975) *The Use of Plastics for Load Bearing and Infill Panels*, University of Surrey Symposium, 1974, Manning Rapley, London.

Reid, A. and O'Brien, T. (1973) Glass fibre reinforced plastics for buildings, *Architects' Journal*, **157** (12), 669-706; **157** (14), 817–826; 157 (18), 1035–1047.

Scott Bader Co. Ltd (1980) *Crystic Polyester Handbook*, Lund Humphries, London.

Scott Bader/Anmac/Fibreglass (1979) Designing with GRP (Conference at Liverpool University 1979), *Building Specification*, November.

Glass-fibre reinforced cement

The material and its advantages

Glass-fibre-reinforced cement is a composite material consisting of ordinary Portland cement, silica sand and water, mixed with alkali-resistant glass fibres. It has been described by Young (1980) as an 'ideal marriage between brittle materials, cement, sand and glass, to produce a tough composite'. At that time, the most common percentage constitution of the material by weight was as follows:

Portland cement	40%
Water	20%
Sand	40%
Glass fibre	5% (for spray techniques)
	3–4% (for premix)

Later formulations included 0–5 % acrylic polymer.

The ultimate strength of glass-fibre-reinforced cement (GRC) is essentially determined by the presence of the fibres, and is therefore dependent upon the glass content, the orientation of the fibres, the degree of cure, and the bonding of the fibres to the cement/sand matrix.

The glass fibre is introduced into the cement mix to carry the tensile forces, thus overcoming the main disadvantage of cement, which is unreliable and has a relatively low tensile strength. The glass content controls the maximum loading that the material can withstand, the impact performance and the durability of the composite. The incorporation of sand

Fig. 3.1 UOP Fragrances, Tadworth, Surrey (architects: Richard Rogers and Renzo Piano).

into the GRC mix helps to reduce shrinkage during drying out and reduces in-service moisture movement.

When GRC was first developed in the late 1960s, after pioneering studies by Dr A. J. Mujumdar at the Building Research Establishment, it was claimed that it would become a widely used form of building cladding. Metallic claddings were not yet fully developed, and GRC promised to combine the best features of precast with less bulk, lighter weight and tighter tolerances.

These benefits led to early uses on prestigious projects such as UOP Fragrances (architects: Richard Rogers and Renzo Piano) at Tadworth in Surrey (Fig. 3.1). As the use of GRC began to increase, some projects experienced problems with micro-cracking, surface shadowing and panel tolerances. The industry did not respond positively to these problems, and GRC fell out of favour with British architects, as they became more interested in the development of metal-faced composite cladding.

Thus in the years since the *Architects' Journal's* detailed coverage of the performance of GRC (Brookes, 1986), UK architects have not used GRC cladding to the extent that was originally predicted. However, GRC continued to be extensively used in continental Europe and in the Middle East, where manufacturers were actively developing their basic formulations, manufacturing methods and cladding systems. European manufacturers include: Dyckerhoff and Widmann in Germany; Besinor, CMEG Creabat, Fiberton in France; Dragados y Construcciones in Spain; and Hibex in The Netherlands. UK manufacturers with an active GRC programme include BCM Contracts, Mouldform, Techcrete (Eire) and Graham Precast.

By reducing the cement : sand ratio (from 1 : 3 to 1 : 1) and by refining the fibre/polymer mix, the amount of daily moisture movement was reduced, resulting in improved surface quality, elimination of microcracking and tighter tolerances. One of the new formulations using Metakaolin pozzolanic aggregate, CemFil 'Star' was marketed by CemFil International Ltd, who claimed that it did not go brittle with age and that it kept its early strength and ductility. Early use of this new formulation includes the Espace Forbin building at Aix en Provence.

As for many new materials, the use of GRC was at first inhibited by lack of experience in use and general rules governing design and adequate codes of practice. At the international congress on glass-fibre-reinforced cement in London, October 1979 (GRCA, 1980), although some speakers complained of the lack of adequate standards, at the same conference M. W. Fordyce and D. Ward described moves towards standard specifications.

A number of major projects have been built using GRC. In the UK, the Credit Lyonnais building in London is still seen as a classic use of GRC moulding, as is the use of composite GRC panels by Richard Rogers at UOP Fragrances Ltd at Tadworth in Surrey. More recent examples include the Grosvenor Hotel and Classic Cinema in Glasgow. A large number of projects have also been built in the Middle East, Spain and Japan, and J. B. Ford (GRCA, 1980) has described

12 projects in the USA using GRC wall panels. Stein (1995) shows several projects in the Middle East.

Design guidance is available describing the properties of glass reinforcement cement. Young (1978) describes the properties of GRC and its methods of manufacture, and gives guidance on the specification and design of such factors as finishes, fixings and joints with reference to a number of case studies. Brookes and Ward (1981) cover developments and feedback from practice. Pilkington (1979) produced design guidance on the use of GRC, which included a detailed description of such properties as its creep and stress rupture, fatigue, density, thermal expansion, thermal conductivity and air and water permeance, with methods of design for determining working stresses, loading, thermal, acoustic and fire performance of a particular design. Information was also given on component testing, quality control and typical specifications.

Designers intending to use the material in complicated shapes or in conjunction with composite insulation core materials should seek further advice from the manufacturers involved. They also may wish to review the recent guidance notes on GRC published by Fachvereingung Faserbeton (FVF), the German GRC trade association. A similar guide is published in the UK by the GRCA entitled *GRC Architectural Components*, and a *Guide to Fixings for Glass Reinforced Cement Claddings* is also available from GRCA.

Production methods

Process methods that have so far been developed for the fabrication of GRC components are **spray** and **premix**. Premix processes are those where the constituents are mixed together into a paste and subsequently formed by casting, press moulding or slip

Fig. 3.2 Typical hand lay-up operation.

forming. Spray processes, in which wet mortar paste and chopped glass fibre are simultaneously deposited from a dual spray-head into a suitable mould, currently account for a large percentage of GRC production.

The properties of GRC premix are inherently different from, and usually inferior to, those of sprayed-up GRC, because more air is introduced into the mixture, and there is less control over the fibre orientation. Thus for cladding panels spray processes are normally used. Three ways of spraying GRC are available:

— manual spray;
— mechanized spray;
— spray-dewater process.

Manual spray

Manual spraying is labour intensive, but offers the designer more flexibility in shape and profile than other methods of fabrication. Using the manual spray the operator moves the spray backwards and forwards across the mould surface until the required thickness of GRC, typically 10–12 mm, as opposed to an average 3–6 mm for GRP, is built up. Greater thickness tends to increase GRC production costs. As with GRP, the material can be built up locally around fixings and inserts, while roller compaction ensures total contact with the mould and removal of entrapped air. Roller compaction should be used after the first 3 mm layer has been sprayed to ensure a good surface finish. For an operator to spray effectively from either side of the mould a dimension of not more than 2 m width is recommended. For greater widths it is possible to erect some sort of working platform above the mould, but this makes spraying difficult, and could affect the quality and cost of production. Figure 3.2 shows manual spraying of GRC wall panels. Robotic spray techniques have also been developed for three-dimensional products.

Mechanized spray

The hand spray can be easily mechanized for the production of simple flat components; the moulds are moved along a conveyor and pass below a boom on which the dual spray-head is mounted, moving to and fro to give uniform thickness and correct fibre distribution through the composite. The mechanical spray thus ensures greater consistency and more uniform thickness than hand spraying. The restriction on width of the mould, as mentioned above, also does not apply. It has been shown possible to automate the manual spray method completely using computer-controlled robot units. However, the cost of mechanized spraying of complicated shapes and window openings becomes prohibitive unless continuous mass productions runs are used, and so far these production methods have not been used for one-off cladding designs in the UK. Post-forming of flat sheets can also be used to produce two-dimensional products.

Spray-dewater process

A variant of the mechanized spray process is the **spray-dewater process**, in which the mould surface consists of a filter membrane through which excess water can be drawn off by vacuum immediately after spraying. The mechanical properties of the laminate are improved by the dewatering process, which produces a denser composite.

A typical automatic spray-dewater plant for the continuous production of flat sheets consists of a mixer and pump conveying the GRC slurry to a slurry spray and glass chopper mounted on a traversing head. A conveyor belt passes the sprayed sheet through a finisher and vacuum box to draw off the excess water. After cutting and trimming, the 'green' sheet so produced can be removed, using a vacuum lift, in its limp state for post-forming into simple shapes. Although such production processes are used in the UK, manufacturers tend to use dewatering processes only for the production of small flat units, such as wall or ceiling tiles, and find the manual spray methods more suitable for complex shapes. However, the increasing use of superplasticizers has reduced the benefits of this process, which has limited application.

Insulated panels

The inclusion of insulation between two skins of GRC is carried out in two main ways, as follows.

—   Panels of polystyrene may be placed in position and then covered with a slurry, or preformed webs of GRC used between the sheets of insulation to stiffen the panel.

—   Suitable foam may be injected between the two preformed skins of GRC. Foams include polyisocyanurate, polyurethane and phenolic. In the last case internal webs of GRC are also used, because the shear performance of the foam is inadequate.

Moulds

Although GRC, being a moulded material, offers the architect great flexibility in shapes and contours to be designed, in practice the types of mould and methods of spraying may restrict the size and shape of the unit. This is particularly true for sandwich panels. As with GRP, the effect of the mould costs on the finished panel is dependent upon complexity, the numbers taken off the mould, and the number of specials required. It is therefore necessary to keep the number of specials to a minimum. Where possible, the basic mould should be adaptable to produce panel variants. For example, at the UOP Fragrances factory, Tadworth, Surrey (architects: Piano and Rogers), various adaptor pieces were inserted in the timber and marine ply moulds to provide the seven panel variants, and detachable pieces were needed to allow moulding of the complex edge shapes.

Most GRC production using the spray method requires anything up to 24 hours before demoulding. Thus the speed of production will be determined by the number of moulds available. Requirements for higher mould utilization have led to developments in rapid-setting types of Portland cement and accelerated dewatering processes.

The number of units to be cast will determine the material from which the mould is made. In general, timber moulds are used for 'short' runs, where a small number of units are required (approximately 30 castings can be obtained from a single mould). For most purposes, moulds in GRP are the most appropriate material, because they are more durable than timber and offer a better standard of surface finish. Steel moulds can be used for long continuous runs.

Using spray production, it is possible to obtain a smooth finish only on the mould side. The non-moulded face will have the textured surface of the compaction roller or a trowelled finish.

Cast or moulded GRC allows for the formation of very intricate surface detailing in cladding panels, as demonstrated on the renovation of existing buildings such as St George's Hospital at Hyde Park Corner and the Grosvenor Hotel in Glasgow. The Woolworth building in New York also makes extensive use of GRC. While it does not offer the aesthetic flexibility of reconstituted stone, it does have an advantage in terms of lower weight and thinner sections.

Typical dimensions of GRC panels are shown in Fig. 3.3.

Finishes

Normally, GRC components would cure to the greyish colour of ordinary Portland cement. White Portland cement has often been used for cladding panels to improve their appearance, but complete uniformity of colour from one panel to another may not be achievable because of variations during manufacture. Panels produced in smooth-surfaced moulds will have a glossy finish on one side only, which tends to accentuate small surface defects and show up the inherent post-curing patchiness of the material. The cement-rich layer at the surface may also show a slight surface crazing. For example, according to Young (1978), panels at the Melrose Centre, Milton Keynes (architects: Colquhoun and Miller) showed that a combination of white cement, a smooth glassy mould surface and the inherent post-curing patchiness of the material and

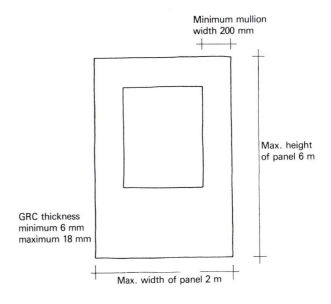

Fig. 3.3 Typical panel dimensions.

slight surface crazing produce an effect not unlike marble.

There are four basic ways in which the colour and texture of GRC can be modified:

- surface treatments and textured moulds;
- pigmented colouring;
- applied paint coatings;
- PVC film.

Surface treatments and textured moulds

As with concrete, some surface treatments can be applied either during moulding using textured moulds or after casting using acid-etching, grit blasting or smooth grinding techniques. These techniques can be particularly valuable in removing any excess cement/sand laitance, and hence can reduce the tendency to crazing. Considerable skill is needed in retaining minimum component thickness after the treatment has been applied. Any textured layers must be considered as surface treatment only, and must not be taken into account in determining the structural performance of the cladding.

Large-aggregate finishes, as used with precast concrete, are not normally recommended, because they have to be embedded in 10–15 mm of cement, making the panels heavier and less manoeuvrable. Normally only aggregate less than 12 mm is used because of the excessive amount of GRC required behind larger aggregate.

Surface finishes of GRC can also be modified using applied acrylics, formed textures, or exposed aggregates. Typically, very fine aggregates may be used, opening up a wide range of aesthetic possibilities, including reclaimed ground glass as the aggregate. High-gloss finishes are possible but expensive; also, these have the disadvantage that any surface irregularity will be emphasized in bright light.

Pigmented colouring

Like precast concrete, coloured panels have been manufactured using pigments and coloured sands, or by adding coloured Metakaolin pozzolanic aggregates. Naturally, the colours tend to be muted and limited in range to softer colours.

Applied paint coatings

As with all cement-based systems, GRC is also subject to moisture movement in that it expands during water uptake and contracts when drying. Great care should therefore be taken in the consideration of any applied coating. Impermeable coatings for external use should generally be avoided, as they can lead to an increased risk of interstitial condensation, particularly with sandwich panels. If the panels are not allowed to 'breathe', then moisture migrating to the surface will cause any impermeable paint to blister or flake.

Proprietary textured permeable finishes, such as those used for coating external masonry, e.g. Muroplast, Sandtex and Glamrock, are often used. Such finishes were used at Heathrow Eurolounge and at Newton Heath Library.

Clear surface coatings of the silicon type, which are particularly useful in protecting the surface of white GRC panels against dirt and fingermarks, can be used without fear of blistering, as they allow the GRC to breathe.

Care must be taken when applying paint coatings, whether in the factory or on site, to ensure that the surface is free from grease or any trace of mould release agent, so that an adequate bond is maintained between the GRC and the paint system base coat.

Some GRC panels have been produced to emulate the aesthetic features of flat metal systems by incorporating a PVC finish. The PVC sheets are either cast in line integrally with the PVC facing or adhesive bonded to the GRC subsequent to moulding. Such panels were used at the Oxford Ice Rink (architects: Nicholas Grimshaw & Partners) (Fig. 3.14) and at the Sheffield Arena (architect: HOK).

Thus coloured panels can be obtained by the use of pigments and coloured sands or by adding coloured Metakaolin. However, these colours are muted and limited in their colour range, and architects may prefer to specify acrylic-based emulsion applied on site or in the factory. High-gloss finishes are possible but expensive. Also, these high-gloss surfaces have the disadvantage that any surface irregularities will be emphasized in bright light.

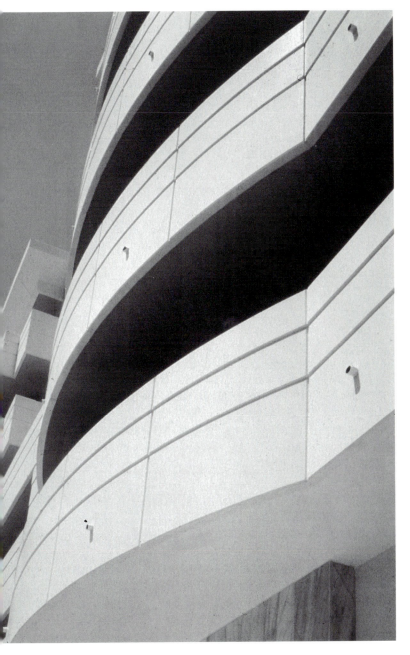

Fig. 3.4 Curved G.R.C. panels..

Performance characteristics

Wind loading

Simplified tables are now available for determining the spanning characteristics of varying thicknesses of GRC in relation to wind loading (Table 3.1). For example, 10–12 mm flat sheets will span 1.0 m under a wind pressure of 1.0 N/m², but sheet of the same thickness can be profiled or ribbed to span up to 4.0 m under the same wind pressure. For greater spans or wind pressure, it may be necessary to design using sandwich construction, ribs or, more commonly today, a stud frame construction.

Thermal characteristics

A 20 mm single-skin GRC construction of approximate density 1800–2100 kg/m³ gives a negligible insulation value, in the region of 5.0 W/m²°C. For improved thermal insulation (up to a U value of 0.7 W/m²°C), it is necessary to incorporate an insulation core into the construction or to incorporate some form of insulation behind a single-skin facade, a method that is finding increasing use in continental Europe. Table 3.2 shows the thermal performance of varying thicknesses of GRC sandwich panels.

Fire performance

In terms of fire performance, GRC is non-combustible when tested to BS 476. Even with an organic paint finish, GRC performs to Class 0 standard when tested in accordance with Part 6. This is generally comparable to metal and precast performance. However, it is important to check the use of polymer additives, because they affect the fire performance of the panel. In terms of fire rating, 1.5 hours fire resistance is claimed by some sandwich panel manufacturers, such as Veldhoen.

Table 3.1 Panel thickness and span

The following tables give a guide to the recommended panel thickness for different panel types.

Single skin flat sheet

Panel span metres	Minimum required GRC thickness, mm		
	0.5 kN/m² Wind Pressure	1.0 kN/m² Wind Pressure	1.5 kN/m² Wind Pressure
0.5	4	6	7
1.0	8	11	14
1.5	12	17	*
2.0	16	*	*

*Use profiling, stiffening ribs or sandwich panel

Profiled single skin (10 mm thick)

For a profiled single skin panel the table below should be used to select the panel design type based on the required span and wind pressure.

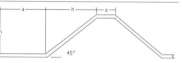

Panel span metres	Wind Pressure 0.5 kN/m² h (mm) × a (mm)	Wind Pressure 1.0 kN/m² h (mm) × a (mm)	Wind Pressure 1.5 kN/m² h (mm) × a (mm)
1.0	50 × 100	50 × 100	50 × 100
1.5	50 × 100	50 × 100	50 × 100
2.0	50 × 100	100 × 150	100 × 150
2.5	100 × 150	100 × 150	100 × 200
3.0	100 × 150	150 × 200	200 × 300
3.5	150 × 200	200 × 300	200 × 300
4.0	200 × 300	200 × 300	Use sandwich panel

Sandwich construction

In selecting parameters for sandwich construction panels, it should be noted that the panel thickness includes two 10 mm thick GRC skins.

Panel span metres	Minimum recommended overall panel thickness, mm		
	Wind Pressure 0.5 kN/m²	Wind Pressure 1.0 kN/m²	Wind Pressure 1.5 kN/m²
*2.0	50	50	50
*2.5	65	65	65
*3.0	70	70	75
*3.5	80	80	95
*4.0	95	95	120
4.5	105	105	145
5.0	115	125	175
5.5	140	145	210
6.0	150	170	245

*Can also use profiled or ribbed single skin GRC

Table 3.2 Thermal performance of varying thicknesses of GRC sandwich panels. Material from BS 5427: 1976 is reproduced by permission of the British Standards Institution, 2 Park Street, London WIA 2BS

Composition of GRC sandwich panel		U-value (W/m²°C)
	GRC 20 mm	5.0
70 mm	GRC 10 mm / PBAC 50 mm / GRC 10 mm	2.0
110 mm	GRC 10 mm / PBAC 100 mm / GRC 10 mm	1.3
100 mm	GRC 10 mm / PBAC 30 mm / Polystyrene 20 mm / PBAC 30 mm / GRC 10 mm	0.9
150 mm	GRC 10 mm / PBAC 50 mm / Polystyrene 30 mm / PBAC 50 mm / GRC 10 mm	0.7

Note: PBAC-polystyrene bead aggregate concrete.

Acoustic performance

A 10 mm single skin of GRC at 20 kg/m² density gives sound reduction indices from 22 dB at 350 Hz to 39 dB at 4000 Hz, or an average of 30 dB over the normal range of frequencies. Even if the single skin is increased to 20 mm, which is beyond the thickness normally recommended, the average reduction indices will increase to only 35 dB. For greater acoustic performance it is possible to specify sandwich construction; however, if it is necessary to connect the outer and inner skins for structural reasons, this will reduce the sound insulation for the whole panel.

Density

A piece of flat GRC 10 mm thick weighs approximately 20 kg/m².

Shrinkage and moisture movement

Like other cement-based materials, GRC exhibits non-reversible shrinkage during the curing process, and long-term moisture movement caused by changes in humidity. The incorporation of 40% silica sand into the matrix reduces both types of shrinkage but, even so, actual movements in use could in theory be 1.5 mm/m. In practice, movement of 1.0 mm/m may be experienced, which is approximately double that of ordinary reinforced concrete. Care has to be taken in the design of fixings to allow for this movement.

Impact loading

GRC is also good at withstanding impact loading. CemFil International quote an impact strength of 10–25 kJ/m² for hand or machine spray products and 10–15 kJ/m² for vibrated cast products.

Types of cladding

Several systems of GRC cladding and roofing have been developed over the past decade, including:

- single-skin cladding or roofing;
- profiled sheeting;
- composite panels with foamed polyurethane;
- cast or moulded products.

In single-skin form, GRC can be mounted onto a metal stud framing (Fig. 3.5). This framing provides support and stiffness against out-of-plane forces, and

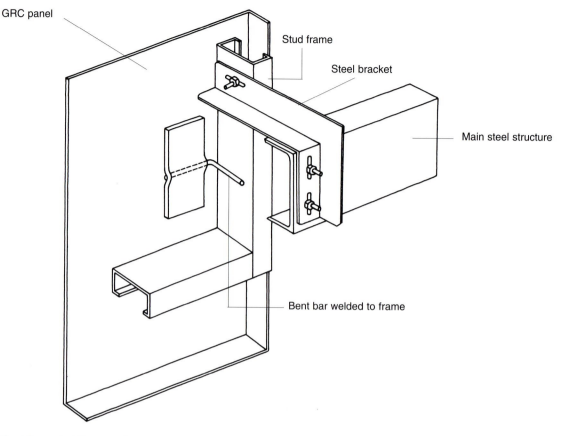

GRC panel

Stud frame

Steel bracket

Main steel structure

Bent bar welded to frame

Fig. 3.5 Fixing method for a stud frame system.

permits expansion and contraction of the GRC skins. This approach has been extensively used in Germany and the USA and increasingly in the UK and continental Europe.

The choice of the type of construction (single skin, profiled or sandwich) will be governed by a combination of requirements that need to be satisfied: fire, thermal, acoustic, weight etc. Table 3.3 shows the relationship between various types of wall construction and the performance requirements for spans, fire resistance and weight, which are usually the most critical.

The total effective depth of large panels can usually be reduced using sandwich construction, as large single-skin panels would require deep stiffening ribs to prevent deflection under load.

In sandwich construction a larger overall thickness than indicated by strength calculations would usually be used to satisfy fire and thermal characteristics and also minimize bowing. This may also be minimized by limiting panel length or width, because the effect is proportional to the square of either dimension; increased panel thickness has a directly beneficial effect in minimizing bowing. Bowing has

Table 3.3 Relationship between wall construction and performance requirements

Wall construction		Maximum recommended span (1.0 kN/m² wind pressure)	Fire resistance BS 476 Part 8	Weight (approximate)
Single skin		Metres	Hours	kg/m²
	Flat GRC 8 mm thick	0.8	None claimed	16
	Flat GRC 12 mm thick	1.1	None claimed	24
	Profiled or ribbed GRC + 50 mm glass-fibre insulation + plasterboard	Up to 4	0.5	40
	Profiled or ribbed GRC + 50 mm glass-fibre insulation +100 mm concrete block	Up to 4	4	100

Increased depth of profile and stiffening ribs increases the spanning capability of the panel

Sandwich construction				
	10 mm GRC 50 mm polystyrene 10 mm GRC	3.0	2	60
Overall panel thickness 70 mm				
	10 mm GRC 60 mm polystyrene 10 mm GRC	3.0	None claimed	46
Overall panel thickness 70 mm				
	10 mm GRC 50 mm PBAC 30 mm polystyrene 50 mm PBAC 10 mm GRC	5.5	4	150
Overall panel thckness 150 mm				

Note: PBAC – polystyrene bead aggregate concrete.

not been a problem in single-skin construction with separate insulation applied on site.

If the panel is required to act as a true sandwich, and for the core to have sufficient shear strength, it is important to form a good bond between the GRC and the insulating core in order to prevent delamination of the core from the skin, which may be caused, in turn, through the bowing of the panel.

Sandwich panels have tended to predominate in the UK. For example, the RACS Superstore, Thanet, Kent (architects: Royal Arsenal Co-operative Society Ltd) is clad with what were claimed at the time of construction to be the largest GRC panels manufactured in Europe. These panels weigh just over 4 t and have thermal insulation of 0.9 W/m^2°C. In overseas contracts, however, this requirement for thermal insulation and other performance requirements were achieved using single-skin construction, ribbed where necessary, with separate insulation applied on site. For example, the Sports and Leisure Centre in Saudi Arabia (architects/consulting engineers: Slater Hodder/Cooper McDonald) uses GRC on the fascia panels to the roof and barrel vaults. This move away from sandwich panels is due partly to the greater thermal stresses and hence bowing problems in hot countries and partly to manufacturing difficulties.

Bridging webs used to give stiffness to larger panels can cause ghosting of the surface finish, as in the case reported by Young (1978) at the UOP Fragrances factory, where, although a special case using a site-applied urethane paint finish, the egg crate construction could be seen on the panel face. Young suggests the most probable explanation is that paint on the insulated skins (130 mm polystyrene) cured at a different rate from that in those areas where webs linked skins and at the edges of window surrounds. However, he also reports (1980) feedback from the Melrose Centre, Milton Keynes, where 77 mm polystyrene core was used with two skins of 6 mm GRC, and no ghosting of stiffening webs occurred. He suggests that this may be because the panels were left as white Portland cement on all surfaces, and because the method of production meant that the insulation was not added until about 2 hours after spraying. The decision to use the non-moulded finish on the outside of the panels may account for the same lack of apparent ghosting on the panels at the Scion Computer Centre, where 50 mm polystyrene core was used.

In order to improve the thermal performance of the panel and, at the same time, improve its fire resistance and stiffness characteristics, multiple sandwich panels of GRC and rigid polystyrene foam have been used (Table 3.2).

Jointing

The techniques used to seal joints in GRC components or panels are similar to those used for precast concrete or GRP. There are essentially four main ways of dealing with joints:

— gaskets;
— baffles in an open-drained joint;
— face sealants;
— cover strips.

Gasket joints

Gaskets are effective only where positive pressure is available to deform or compress them. A typical joint incorporates a top-hat section with captive nut to pull back a metal cover strip against a neoprene gasket. Advantage can be taken of the quality of the edge profile, which is normally possible in GRC, to use push-in fir-cone gaskets, as used, for example, at the UOP Fragrances factory (architects: Piano and Rogers) (Fig. 3.6). These gaskets incorporate barbed legs, which

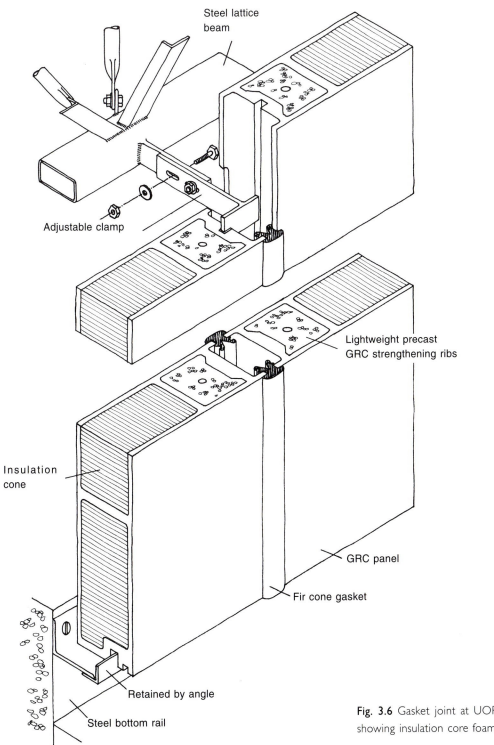

Steel lattice
beam

Adjustable clamp

Insulation
cone

Lightweight precast
GRC strengthening ribs

GRC panel

Fir cone gasket

Retained by angle

Steel bottom rail

Fig. 3.6 Gasket joint at UOP Fragrances factory,
showing insulation core foamed between skins.

can be pushed into position in the joint. One problem in using such gaskets is that the moulded GRC nibs to receive the gasket have only one mould face, and however well the back face is compacted, minor variations in thickness will occur, which can cause points of weakness for an effective weatherproof seal. These nibs can be wrapped in tape to take up any tolerances in surface defects resulting from manufacture, in order to gain a tight fit before applying the compression gasket. The UOP Fragrances factory also used a push-in gasket on the inside face; some difficulty may be experienced in sealing past the adjustable clamps in such a detail.

Another problem with gasket joints is that they depend upon extremely tight tolerance in joint size, and may only really work in conjunction with a system of adjustable fixing devices. Typical permissible joint range clearances are 5–10 mm. The use of slotted holes and T-clamps at UOP Fragrances resulted in precise location of panels, allowing the use of this method of gasket jointing even at the corner detail. Direct glazing of windows into GRC is also possible using neoprene gaskets.

Open-drained joints

One of the requirements of an open-drained joint is that the baffle groove is deep enough to accommodate the baffle at the maximum and minimum joint ranges. Typical baffle groove depths are 30 mm. Such deep grooves are difficult to form during GRC manufacture. Furthermore, it is not always easy to fix the baffle strip at the head of the joint. For these reasons this form of joint is not often used for GRC panels.

Mastic sealants

Various mastic sealants, including polysulphides, polyurethane and silicone rubbers, have been used, but their success depends upon good surface prepa-

ration and the use of correct primers. The sealant surface may be exposed to ultraviolet light, and its long-term attributes are therefore questionable. Manufacturers' recommendations for sealants must be closely followed at all times. Sealants designed to bond to smooth surfaces should be specified, and care should be taken to ensure that any silicone face sealer to the panel is not carried round the edges of the panel, as this inhibits adhesion of the sealant.

Cover strips

Although in theory it is possible to disguise the joint using a cover strip, these are not often used, partly because they are not normally visually acceptable, and partly because the design of the intersection between vertical and horizontal cover strips makes it almost impossible to maintain weather tightness.

Top-hat sections are used for fixing back foamed GRC panels onto a structural framework (Fig. 3.7), and proprietary methods can be used for secret fixing (Fig. 3.8).

Fixings

Fixing methods using angle cleats and dowel fixings are similar to those used for precast concrete. Glass-fibre-reinforced cement panels are best supported at the base and restrained at the top; intermediate fixings should be avoided. Typical fixings for fixing panels back to their supporting framework are shown in Fig. 3.9.

It is most important that allowances are made for the thermal, moisture and any structural movements of the GRC, which are approximately double those of precast concrete. For cladding panels these provisions for movement are usually accommodated in the top restraint fixings in the form of slotted or oversize holes (Fig. 3.10). Frictionless washers or

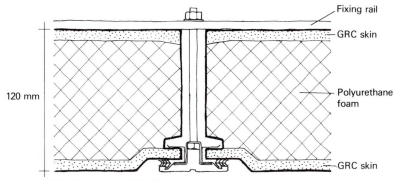

120 mm

Fixing rail

GRC skin

Polyurethane foam

GRC skin

Total *U* value 0.23 W/m²°C

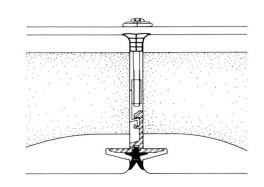

Fig. 3.8 Proprietary method of secretly fixing GRC back onto a structural framework.

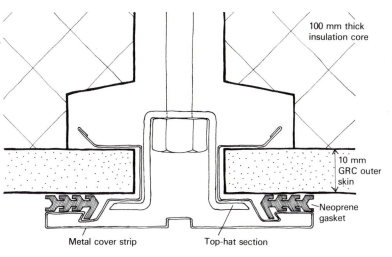

100 mm thick insulation core

10 mm GRC outer skin

Neoprene gasket

Metal cover strip   Top-hat section

Fig. 3.7 Top-hat section for fixing foamed GRC panel back onto a structural framework.

bearing pads of neoprene or polytetrafluoroethylene (PTFE) and spacer tubes, or a resilient rubber bush or spring, must be incorporated to allow the component parts to slide and move (Fig. 3.11). If a fixing is tightened on site without such devices, the forces will be transferred into the panel, leading to bolt failure or local failure of the GRC.

Cast-in fixings should be encapsulated in a zone of good-quality GRC with a minimum width of 12 times the bolt diameter, and a minimum of six times the bolt diameter between the centre of the bolt fixing and the edge of the panel (Fig. 3.12). Only cast-in fixings should be used for structural connections. Site-drilled holes are adequate for secondary fixings, although it is usual even in this case to provide plastic area fixings to allow a degree of dimensional flexibility.

Where single-skin construction in GRC is used, the panels can be fixed back to the secondary framing using cleats mounted on the stiffening ribs. Figure 3.13 shows a typical example, where the panel is fixed to a horizontal rail supported by steel uprights at intervals along the perimeter of the façade.

Panel dimensions and tolerances

Although in theory there is no real restriction on the length of panel, in practice this is normally limited to 4–6 m because of problems of lifting, handling and fixing of units. Maximum widths of panels depend upon the method of production. For manual spraying this is normally limited to 2 m. Where windows are incorporated within a panel, a minimum mullion width of 200 mm is recommended. Glass-fibre-reinforced cement single-skin thickness is minimum 6 mm and maximum 18 mm for sprayed material. For premix material the minimum thickness is normally 10 mm, with no upper limit within reason.

Tolerances in panels are similar to those used for precast concrete, but should not exceed ±3 mm for small panels.

Handling of units on site and storage

Because of the ease with which GRC can be formed in a variety of shapes, it is not uncommon to avoid the potentially troublesome eaves detail by cranking or curving the panels at their junction with the roof (Fig. 3.4). Such panels were used at the fire station at the National Exhibition Centre and at Heathrow Eurolounge. Special equipment may be necessary for handling such units on site, and care must also be taken in designing the fixing devices for lifting to ensure that these do not show on the outside face. Highly profiled panels are also difficult to store and transport, and cranked panels will twist and distort if stacked unsupported on edge (Fig. 3.15).

Also, large upstands and long unsupported ends tend to settle when in their 'green' state, and care must be taken during manufacture and storage to avoid sagging of unsupported ends. If this is not done, problems can occur in controlling the size of

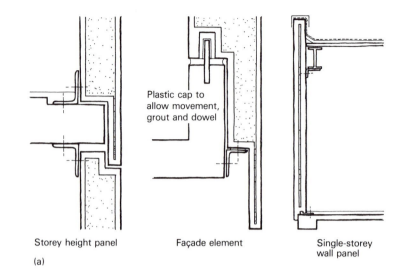

Storey height panel   Façade element   Single-storey wall panel

(a)

Plastic cap to allow movement, grout and dowel

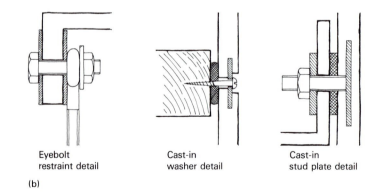

Eyebolt restraint detail   Cast-in washer detail   Cast-in stud plate detail

(b)

Fig. 3.9 Typical fixings using GRC: (a) sandwich construction fixings; (b) single skin fixings.

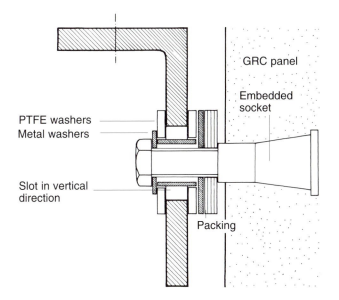

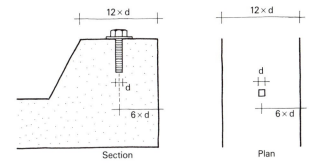

Fig. 3.10 Slotted fixings to allow movement at top of panel.

Fig. 3.12 Minimum cover to cast-in fixings.

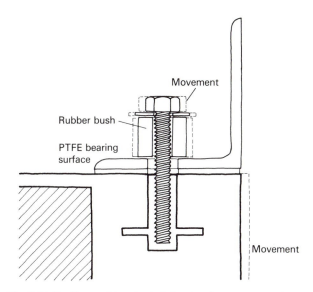

Fig. 3.11 Resilient rubber bush fixing to allow movement.

joints between panels because of difficulties in ensuring alignment of panels during erection.

Repair on site

Although it is possible for specialist contractors to repair minor defects on site using manually applied cement/sand slurry where structural damage has taken place in the form of large holes and the fibre/cement bond has been broken down, panels should be removed and returned to the factory for repair under closer quality workmanship control, or preferably replaced by a new panel. Panels with surface texture treatments should be resprayed to avoid any patchiness occurring on the panel face where the repair has taken place.

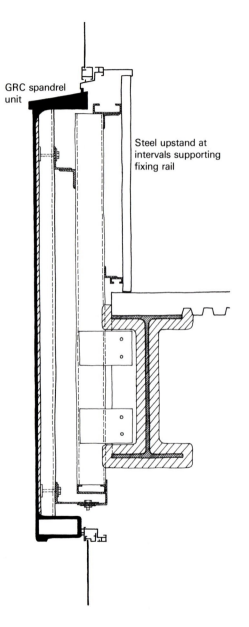

GRC spandrel
unit

Steel upstand at
intervals supporting
fixing rail

Fig. 3.13 Example of single-skin GRC spandrel panel detail on metal framework.

Conclusion

If GRC systems have a persistent fault, it tends to lie in relatively unsophisticated detailing between the panels and in the details relating to the panels to adjacent windows, doors, curtain walling and louvre systems. Clearly GRC systems have not kept pace with metal-based cladding systems (see Chapter 5), with their interchangeable panels and sophisticated crossover joints.

The lack of sophisticated detailing explains why, even in continental Europe, GRC systems are predominantly specified on factories, middle market offices, schools and sports facilities, which have a need for the performance characteristics of the material. Architects working on projects that have higher aesthetic requirements have found the detailing unsuitable.

Manufacturers now, however, seem more interested in taking this problem on board, especially in the light of the downturn in the traditional markets experienced over the past three years. Advances are being made in cutting and forming the edge of the material to allow more sophisticated arrangements. Other opportunities include the inclusion of EPDM or neoprene gaskets mounted within the panel edge. Some manufacturers are developing horizontal panel arrangements as well as a fully integrated system of panels and windows.

Given improvements in GRC technology, which are backed up by a strong track record of successful projects in Europe, the performance advantages of modern GRC may warrant reconsideration. In terms of costs, the installed costs of GRC sandwich constructions average from £80 to £150/m^2, which is roughly equivalent to some flat metal sandwich constructions and about twice the cost of corrugated metal constructions. Costs for moulded GRC constructions are 20–30% more expensive than those

Fig. 3.14 Oxford Ice Rink (architects: Nicholas Grimshaw & Partners).

for equivalent precast concrete, depending on its complexity and the quantities involved. However, GRC may be more cost-effective than precast when savings on superstructure are considered.

It can be seen that the glass fibres constitute only a small percentage by weight of the material, and although, for example, fibres for GRC (Cem-fil) cost twice as much as fibres for GRP (£2000/t in 1981), the resultant material cost of a total 12 mm composite is only approximately half that of the material needed for an equivalent GRP composite. Having

said that, of course, the material costs represent only a small percentage of the total costs, which will include overheads on production for more complicated panel shapes.

Glass-fibre-reinforced cement can be seen as an alternative to ordinary reinforced concrete in respect to its weather resistance, non-combustibility and low thermal movement. Advantage can be taken of its higher strength-to-weight ratio than those of other cementitious materials to produce strong, fire-resistant yet lightweight claddings. (Its strength-to-weight ratio is, however, less than that of GRP or metals.) Inevitably, though, it is compared with GRP in respect to its method of manufacture and its resultant ability to be formed into a variety of shapes.

Cement, when reinforced with glass fibre, produces precast elements much thinner – typically 10 mm – than would be possible with traditional steel-reinforced precast concrete, where 30 mm or more concrete cover to the steel is essential as protection against corrosion. Thinner sections are also made possible by the low water : cement ratio of the material, the lack of coarse aggregate, and its low permeability. As a result, panels of equal strength and function of precast concrete can be produced with thinner sections and therefore less weight.

In conclusion, it appears that GRC can offer benefits on projects where the physical characteristics of the building can enhance the performance of the building. On very complex projects, which require very sophisticated detailing and integration of many components, GRC is probably unsuitable at present, although promising advances are being pursued.

References and further reading

Brookes, A. J. (1986) Element design guide, external walls, GRC. *Architects' Journal*, **184** (33), 43–48.

Brookes, A. J. (1993) GRC cladding is looking good. *Architects' Journal*, **198** (September), 25–27.

Brookes, A. J. and Ward, M.A. (1981) The art of construction – GRC claddings. *Architects' Journal*, **174** (28), 127–136.

BRE (1974) *Glass fibre reinforced cement*, BRE Current Paper CP 79/74, Building Research Establishment, Garston.

BRE (1976) *A study of the properties of Cem-fil OPC composites*, BRE Current Paper CP 38/76, Building Research Establishment, Garston.

BRE (1978) *GRC*, BRE Digest No. 216, HMSO, London.

BRE (1979) *Properties of GRC: ten-year results*, BRE Internal Paper IP 36/79, Building Research Establishment, Garston.

GRCA (1980) *The Developing Success of GRC*, Proceedings of the International Congress on Glassfibre Reinforced Cement, London, 10–12 October, 1979, Glass Fibre Reinforced Cement Association, London.

GRCA (1995) *Specification for the manufacture of glassfibre reinforced cement*, Glass Fibre Reinforced Cement Association, London.

Litherland, K. L., Oakley, D. R. and Proctor, B. A. (1980) The use of accelerated ageing procedures to predict the long-term strength of GRC composites. *Cement and Concrete Research*, **2** (3), 455–466.

Pilkington (1979) *Cem-fil GRC. Design Guide*, 2nd edn, Pilkington Bros Ltd, St Helens, Merseyside.

Proctor, B. A. (1980) Properties and performance of GRC, in *Proceedings of Fibrous Concrete Symposium 1980*, Concrete Society, London, pp. 69–86.

Stein, C. (1995) *Architectural criteria for glass fibre reinforced concrete*, Paper for GRCA 1995 Congress.

Young, J. (1978) GRC – a briefing guide to architects. *Architects' Journal*, 15 February; 8 March; 29 March; 19 April.

Young, J. (1980) *Designing with GRC*, Architectural Press, London.

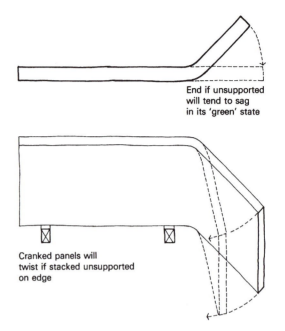

Fig. 3.15 Cranked panels need supporting to avoid distortion during curing.

End if unsupported will tend to sag in its 'green' state

Cranked panels will twist if stacked unsupported on edge

Formed metal including profiled metal

This chapter discusses steel or aluminium sheeting, profiled, pressed or formed to impart stiffness and hence strength to thin and otherwise flexible skins.

Forming of metal

Forming of sheet metal can be carried out in four different ways (Fig. 4.1):

—   brake pressing (or folding);
—   rolling;
—   stamping;
—   deep drawing.

The size and shape of the final product is influenced by the type of production method used.

Brake pressing

Bending of metal sheet in its cold state is a relatively simple process, using a **brake press**, and once a sheet of metal (usually 2–4 mm thick) has been cut at the corners, it can be formed into a tray using a V-shaped bending tool (Fig. 4.2) and the corners welded. In order to do this the sheets must first be cut at their corners prior to brake pressing (Fig. 4.3). Today, brake presses can be computer controlled to produce a wide variety of edge profiles (Fig. 4.4). The size of the panel produced in this way is limited only by the size of the sheet and the length of the brake press (maximum length 6 m). Finishes, such as anodizing, would be applied to these panels after fabrication.

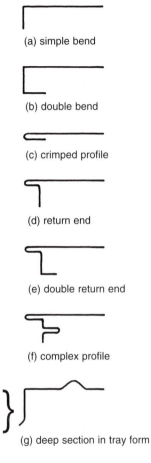

(a) simple bend

(b) double bend

(c) crimped profile

(d) return end

(e) double return end

(f) complex profile

deep draw

(g) deep section in tray form

Fig. 4.1 Methods of forming metal to shape.

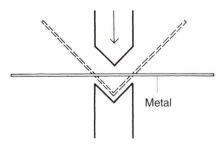

Metal

Fig. 4.2 V-shaped bending tool.

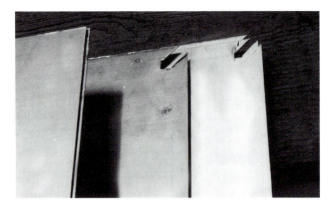

Fig. 4.3 Sheets cut at corners prior to brake pressing.

Rolling

This is normally carried out on a continuous line, either by rolling direct from coil (see 'Steel profiled cladding' p. 90) or by rolling separate sheets. There is no limit to the length of the final product other than that governed by handling or transport (normally 13 m). Simple rolling lines are possible for thinner gauges of metal (up to 1 mm), but more complex profiles for long-span cladding need fixed-stand machines (Fig. 4.5).

Metal stamping

Pressing of sheet metal in one operation is more difficult, and the panels formed in this manner in the UK are normally restricted to 2 m × 1 m. Such panels were produced for the parapet units at the Brunel Centre by Dowty Boulton Paul Ltd, and are typical of panels formed by metal-forming techniques (Fig. 4.6). These techniques are normally associated with the automobile industry, where the cost of the stamp can be amortized over a large number of identical units (Fig. 4.7). The steel panels for the Milton Keynes factory Kiln Farm (architects: Milton Keynes Development Corporation) were also stamped out in one operation (Fig. 4.8). Aluminium sheets were stamped out for the

Fig. 4.4 Brake press.

Herman Miller extension, Bath (architects: Nicholas Grimshaw Partnership), 2.4 m × 1.2 m, by the Kinain workshop. The panel can be stamped as a 'tray' in one operation, as against brake pressing, which can form only one edge at a time (Fig. 4.9). With large panels, it is normal to stamp profiles and then brake press to form edges. Details of the panel joint are shown in Figure. 4.10.

Deep drawing

Where panels need to be pressed in three dimensions this can be done by **deep drawing** techniques. For example, panels at the Federal Technical College, Lausanne,

Fig. 4.5 Typical rolling line.

Fig. 4.6 Brunel Centre, Swindon (architects: Douglas Stephen/Building Design Partnership).

Fig. 4.7 Stamping of metal in one operation, normally associated with automobile industry.

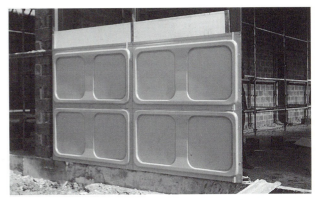

Fig. 4.8 Stamped panels at Milton Keynes.

Switzerland (architects: Zweifel and Strickler), were drawn into a three-dimensional shape by Schmidlin (Fig. 4.11). The 1.8 m × 1.2 m pressed panels for the Sainsbury Centre were produced by TIC Superform by deep-drawing them round a shape using a special alloy of superplastic aluminium.

This proved to be a costly and difficult operation because of the depth of the panels (100 mm), and similar panels at Gatwick Airport North Piers and the Financial Times building, London, were produced with smaller reveals (20–40 mm) (Fig. 4.12).

Profiled metal cladding and roof decking

Definitions

Steel Construction Institute, previously Constrado, (1980) on profiled steel cladding defines **cladding** as:

The external envelope of the building which normally carries no loading beyond its own weight plus the loads imposed by snow, wind and during maintenance. It is the term used when the steel sheet (coated or uncoated) is exposed to the elements. Cladding for walls is sometimes known as

walling or siding and cladding for roofs is generally known as roof sheeting or roof cladding.

and **roof decking** as:

The part of the envelope, on the roof, which supports insulation and waterproofing plus its own weight, plus imposed loads resulting from snow, wind, maintenance and sometimes access. The steel sheet usually forms the inner layer and is not exposed to the elements, unlike roof cladding.

Profiled steel and aluminium sheets are available in sinusoidal, symmetrical and asymmetrical trapezoidal profiles. According to the PSA Method of Building Guide (1979), these can be defined (Fig. 4.13) as:

- **sinusoidal** – where crests and troughs are symmetrical and have the shape of a sine curve;
- **symmetrical trapezoidal** – where crests and troughs are the same width, and the sloping sections are at a constant angle;
- **asymmetrical trapezoidal** – where crests and troughs are unequal in width. The section can be used with either surface outside provided the organic coating is on the correct side.

The industry

Steel profiled cladding

Coiled steel sheet is manufactured in the UK only by the British Steel Corporation (BSC), which supplies it in three main versions:

—   organic coated on a galvanized substrate as in Colorcoat and Stelvetite;
—   galvanized only to BS 2989 for 3 in corrugated sheets to BS 3083 : 1980;
—   undercoated (black steel) to BS 1449 for others to apply their own metallic or organic coatings.

Although BSC Profiles has its own fabricating works at Aycliffe, Darlington, in most cases it supplies the coiled sheet for rolling into profiles by other manufacturers. Most manufacturers sell their rolled products to specialist fixing contractors.

Some manufacturers claim to roll profiles of steel, taking advantage of modern steel processing methods, to attain a higher yield strength of 320–550 N/mm². However, high-tensile steels do not reduce deflection for any given profile or loading, and therefore the spans cannot be increased for deflection-controlled sheets. Thus if deflection is the criterion then high-tensile steel offers no real advantage, but if strength is the criterion then spans can be increased.

Although in the UK coiled steel, with its factory-applied finish, comes mainly from one source, namely BSC, it can sometimes be confusing to the specifier that the same finish, e.g. Plastisol, can be called by different names, e.g. Colourclad or Everclad, depending on the fabricator's description of its particular product range.

Similarly, in considering finishes, it is not always clear which coatings are applied before forming (e.g. BSC Plastisol) and which are applied after forming

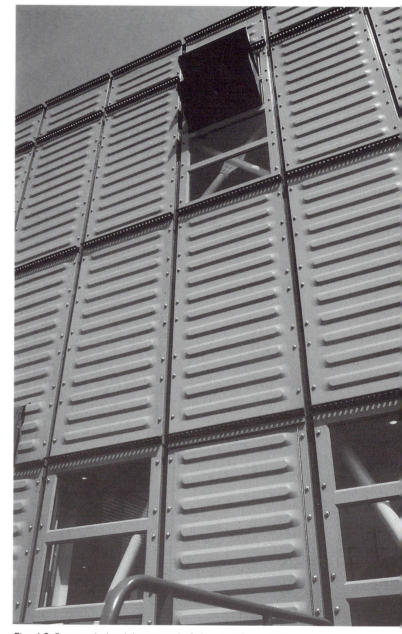

Fig. 4.9 Stamped aluminium panels 2.4 m × 1.2 m at Herman Miller extension, Bath.

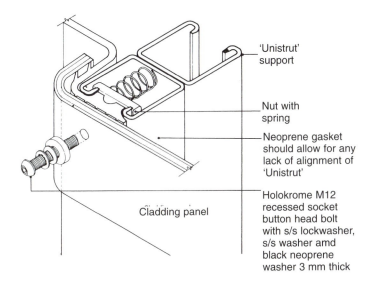

'Unistrut' support

Nut with spring

Neoprene gasket should allow for any lack of alignment of 'Unistrut'

Cladding panel

Holokrome M12 recessed socket button head bolt with s/s lockwasher, s/s washer amd black neoprene washer 3 mm thick

Fig. 4.10 Detail of panels at Herman Miller, Bath.

Fig. 4.11 Deep drawing of complex sections and trays.

Fig. 4.12 Panels by Superform Aluminium at Financial Times building.

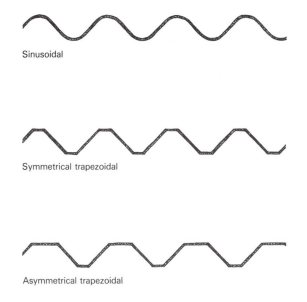

Sinusoidal

Symmetrical trapezoidal

Asymmetrical trapezoidal

Fig. 4.13 Terminology of profiles.

(e.g. Bacocolour – aluminium sheets only), and what are the advantages and disadvantages of each.

Aluminium profiled cladding

All aluminium sheet manufactured in the UK and used for cladding buildings is produced by British Alcan Ltd, which supplies it either finished or plain, to have a finish applied by others.

In other countries, mainly Sweden, it is possible to produce aluminium by other methods of production such as continuous cast coil, and in this way some foreign manufacturers (e.g. Granges Essem) claim that they can produce alloys of greater tensile strength and therefore, for the same span, reduce the thickness (and thus cost) of their material. However, as with steel, these materials are likely to be more expensive than the UK-based product.

Both steel and aluminium offer a wide variety of sharper (trapezoidal) profiles, and can be used horizontally or vertically with patent bending processes available for specially formed corner junctions. The use of horizontal metal sheeting at the IBM offices at Greenford (Fig. 4.14) (architects: Foster Associates), for example, encouraged other architects to use profiled metal sheeting in a similar manner. The selection of either steel or aluminium may be a personal choice. Aluminium is nominally more expensive but, on the other hand, is lighter and therefore, in theory, needs less framing. In practice, because the actual difference is 1.5 kg/m², this makes no difference to the framing in most cases. Maybe the specifier is influenced by steel being, in theory, more susceptible to rusting at the edges of the sheets. In truth, the choice probably rests on the types of finishes available or even the standard of technical back-up service provided by the manufacturers.

Fig. 4.14 IBM offices, Greenford (architects: Foster Associates).

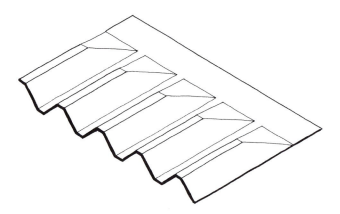

Fig. 4.15 Tapering close-profile flashings available in aluminium.

Profiles

Profiled aluminium sheets to BS 4868 are produced in depths of 8–38 mm and 38–50 mm; however, there are many more trapezoidal profiles produced between 8 mm and 90 mm profile depth, as illustrated in the manufacturers' catalogues. For a complete table of all profiles, see PSA Method of Building Group (1979).

Profiled steel sheets are available up to about 13 m long with cover widths up to 100 mm in stock lengths. Trapezoidal sections are usually made in lengths to order. Sinusoidal sections are available in stock lengths. The profiles of sinusoidal sections are defined in BS 3083 and CP 143 : Part 10.

Sinusoidal profiled steel sheets to BS 3083 are produced in depths of 19 mm. However, there are many more trapezoidal profiles produced up to 100 mm deep, as illustrated in the manufacturers' catalogues.

Architects often require a tapering closed profile section (Fig. 4.15), particularly where sheets abut window details. These can easily be produced in aluminium, but are more difficult in steel. Some steel tapering pieces are available, but they are normally small profiles and may be limited in cover width.

Corner flashing details and profiles are also an important consideration. Some curved eaves and round corners are now available in metal to match the main sheeting (Fig. 4.16).

There has also been an increased interest shown by architects in recent years in the curved forms possible in profiled sheets. Trapezoidal aluminium profiles can be fully or partly curved in their length by British Alcan to a minimum radius of 3000 mm. Tighter radii can be produced using crimped profiles such as those developed by Ash and Lacey as Floclad. Initially a process for steel, it has now been licensed to British Alcan for aluminium profiles.

Design guidance

As well as the manufacturers' own design manuals with specific data provided on such factors as loadings, there are a number of publications offering guidance on the specification of profiled cladding. These include the following.

PSA Method of Building Guide

This includes definitions, and gives safe temperature ranges and estimates of durability for different finishes. It is intended to help the designer to evaluate the existing manufacturers' products by providing comparative tables of profiles for all types of profiled cladding. It also includes application details (PSA Method of Building Group, 1979).

CEGB Guide

This includes recommendations on construction, weatherproofing, fixings, loadings and strength, appearance, durability and other performance factors (CEGB, 1970).

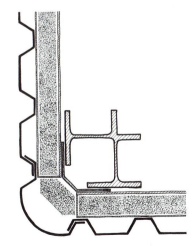

Fig. 4.16 Typical curved eaves and round corners.

Metal Roof Deck Association

This gives codes of design and technical requirements of roof decking (Metal Roof Deck Association, 1970).

British Standards

In addition to the various standards listed later for specific types of cladding and their finishes, BS 5427 : 1976 *Code of practice for performance and loading criteria for profiled sheeting in building* offers general guidance on all types of profiled sheeting (BSI, 1976).

In addition, some manufacturers' design manuals provide application details with typical solutions for corner, head and sill details.

Method of manufacture

In the UK, aluminium is produced by the electrolytic reduction of alumina, from which two types of alloy are made, principally with magnesium, silicon and manganese. These can be hot or cold rolled to form flat sheets or coils.

Steel is made from iron, which is processed with additives such as carbon and manganese to give it added toughness and durability. It is rolled into flat sheets or coils, and is usually given a protective zinc coating in a hot-dip bath. The sheet may then be profiled or cut for site painting or, more usually, given a liquid or bonded coating before profiling and cutting.

Sheet steel and aluminium coil are supplied to the rolling mill for coating and rolling (Fig. 4.17). A typical coating line for sheet steel would consist of the following parts:

Galvanizing plant

Black steel is de-coiled, continuously cleaned and pre-treated prior to zinc coating. A thickness of zinc coating is controlled to the requisite tolerance by means of high-pressure air, which removes the excess zinc. After

galvanizing and cooking, the strip is re-coiled.

Coating line

De-coil strip. To maintain continuous operation successive coils are stitch welded; strip is held in a catenary form to give maximum area for vaporization of the solvents to occur. Time to allow this operation to be completed is provided by means of an accumulator system at the feed ends of the line.

Pretreatment

Remove oil, grease and surface residues by degreasing and zinc passivation with intervening water wash and scrub.

Precoating

A solvent-based primer is applied to both sides of the strip by means of a reverse roll coater.

First oven

The sheet is now suspended (under tension) in a large oven (temperature 260 °C), in which it moves at a maximum speed of 30 m/min. Electronic signalling ensures a nearly constant catenary for the strip so that the vaporization of solvents from the coatings can take place. These solvents are incinerated to prevent atmospheric pollution. The heat generated from the combustion of these solvents is returned via a heat exchanger to preheat the fresh air circulating in the ovens.

Base coat or top coat application

The principal coating is now applied using rubber rollers if both sides of the sheet are to be painted. A second oven then cures this coat. Electronic signalling of the approach of the stitched joint enables the operative to raise the paint applicator rolls to avoid damage to the roller surface by the joint.

The speed of the sheet through the second oven controls the overall speed of the line. It is dictated by

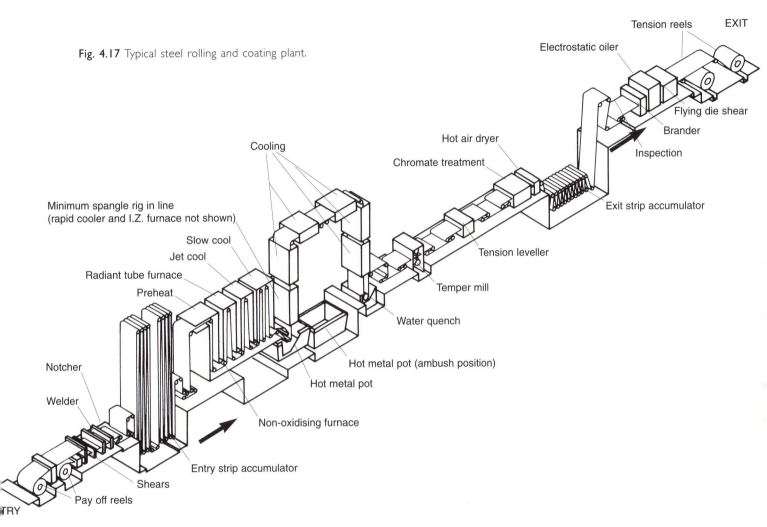

Fig. 4.17 Typical steel rolling and coating plant.

tensioning rollers, which control the catenary in the second oven to ensure that the sheet is suspended correctly and is evenly heated on both sides of the sheet.

An accumulator allows a 1.5 min delay at the end of the line, and a steering mechanism is provided to ensure that the sheet is straight in the line. A back-tension device allows re-coiling of the sheet, and at this stage prepainted sheets can be fed into the line for embossing if required. Sheets are re-coiled prior to being fed into the rolling mill.

Roll form line

The rolling mill consists of a series of adjustable rollers through which the flat sheets are progressively formed into profiled forms. In some cases it is possible to provide lateral profiling by means of a special roller (Fig. 4.18). Sheets can be cut to length before or after profiling. Typical manufacturing deviation on the width of the sheet is ±2 mm.

In forming the painted steel or aluminium strip some faults can occur, such as micro-cracking, fluting, bows or twists. Fluting is a pattern of kinks that occur at the ends of the sheet during rolling. Pre-cut sheets of high-tensile steel are vulnerable to this problem. It can also be caused by excessive amounts of nitrogen in the rolled strip, which may need stretch levelling prior to rolling. Bows and twists can also occur with poor rolling.

To avoid micro-cracking, MacGregor (1981) recommends that the minimum bend radius should be four times the sheet thickness for aluminium and eight times for galvanized steel.

Relevant standards

Steel sheeting

Profiled steel sheets are available in sinusoidal, symmetrical and asymmetrical trapezoidal profiles. Sinusoidal sheets, where the crests and troughs are symmetrical and have the shape of a sine curve, are to BS 3083 : 1988 *Hot dipped galvanized corrugated steel sheets for general purposes* (Tables I and II), and the application of these sheets is covered in CP 143 Part 10 : 1973. However, the majority of architects in the UK specifying precoated steel sheeting are selecting trapezoidal profiles from the manufacturers' catalogues, and refer to BS 5427 : 1976 *Code of practice for performance and loading criteria for profiled sheeting in building.*

BS 3083 : 1988 for hot-dipped galvanized sheets defines the type of zinc coating and tolerances on the size of the sheets. Profiles are made from galvanized sheet steel with or without organic coating, or to BS 1449 Part 1 : 1991 when they are not pregalvanized. The usual quality is Z1, and it is recommended that this has a guaranteed yield stress of 220 N/mm^2, although some manufacturers would claim that they exceed this.

The application for sinusoidal hot-dipped galvanized sheets is given in CP 143 Part 10 : 1973, which

Fig. 4.18 Lateral profiling can be produced by means of a special roller.

deals with materials, design considerations, application, inspection and maintenance. Some information on handling, working, storage and installation is also given in BS 5427 : 1976. Manufacturers' own catalogues would offer the specifier clearer instructions on these matters. Some associations such as the National Federation of Roofing Contractors do offer their own design guidance for the application of profiled sheet metal roofing and cladding.

Standard flashings are supplied by cladding contractors, and should be of zinc to BS 849 : 1939 and not less than 0.8 mm, or lead to BS1178 : 1982 not less than BS code number 4 (20 kg/m). Fixings should be to BS 1494 Part 1 : 1964.

Aluminium sheeting

British Standard 4868 : 1972 *Profiled aluminium sheet for building* relates only to those sheets for which the aluminium alloy has been manufactured in accordance with BS EN 485 governing the wrought aluminium and aluminium alloys.

Profiles, dimensions and cover widths are described in BS 4868 : 1972, which specifies requirements for materials, a limited range of profiles, dimensions and finish. Unfortunately, this refers only to a very limited range of profiles (mainly sinusoidal). Trapezoidal profiles are generally preferred by architects as they are generally crisper and can produce sharp shadow lines, which are useful for breaking up large surfaces. One of the weaknesses of the present standard is that because it includes only a small range of such profiles it therefore excludes most aluminium sheets, which are produced to profile classes not included in the standard.

Similarly, the code of practice (CP 143 Part 15 : 1973) giving recommendations for the installation of aluminium relates in its title to both sheet roof and wall coverings, but in fact refers mainly to its application on roofs and gutters. It also relates to only one alloy, NS3, and is therefore not appropriate to all situations. Brief mention is made of the storage and protection of aluminium sheets, but cross-strappings during unloading and timber cross-battens for stacking are not mentioned, nor are there any limits given for the height of the stack. Manufacturers' own guidance would offer the specifier clearer instructions on these matters.

Fixings should comply with the requirements of BS 1494 Part 1 : 1964, showing various fixings for sheet roof and wall coverings. BS 4174 : 1972 gives the same range of requirements for self-tapping screws and metallic drive screws.

Durability

Perhaps the most serious weakness of the existing standards is that they appear to offer no real assurance to the specifier over the durability and life to first maintenance of these organic coatings.

Some information on durability of surface finish and details of life to first maintenance for factory and site-applied finishes on aluminium is contained in Appendix E of BS 5427 : 1976, which is a general code of practice for performance and loading criteria for profiled weathering sheeting in a range of materials used in building (Table 4.1). There is some disagreement within the industry on the basis for the data given in such tables, and the code states that the data should be regarded only as a guide, and that the manufacturer should be consulted for each specific application and environment.

Allowable tolerance in matching colours also needs clarification. BS 4904 : 1978 *External cladding colours for building purposes* relates colours in terms of hue, greyness and weight, but no mention is made in this document of the performance of different colours, or indeed of their relative colour fastness. Matching is

Table 4.1 General characteristics of factory- and site-applied finishes on aluminium and primed hot-dip zinc-coated mild steel

Surface finish on steel	Characteristics				
	Scratch resistance	Stain resistance	Colour fastness	Weathering	Chalking resistance
1. Solution vinyl					
Min 20 μm vinyl chloride acetate copolymer	G	M	P	P	P
2. Alkyds					
Min 20 μm alkyd and oil-free polyester	G	G	G	G	M
3. Acrylics					
Min 20 μm thermosetting and thermoplastic acrylic copolymers	G	G	G	M	M
4. PVC Organosol					
Min 20 μm siliconised versions of acrylics, alkyds and oil-free polyesters	G	M	P	P	P
5. Silicone enamels					
Min 20 μm siliconised versions of acrylics, alkyds and oil-free polyesters	G	G	G	M	G
6. Fluoropolymers (liquid applied)					
Min 20 μm PVF and PVF$_2$	G	E	E	E	E
7. Fluoropolymers (film applied)					
Min 20 μm PVF and PVF$_2$	G	E	E	E	E
8. Vinasol					
Min 75 μm film organic coating PVC homopolymer	G	M	M	G	M
9. Plastisol					
Min 175 μm film organic coating PVC homopolymer liquid-applied	G	G	G	G	G
10. PVC film					
Min 175 μm film organic coating PVC homopolymer-bonded laminates	G	G	G	G	G
11. Acrylic film					
Min 50 μm film high molecular weight acrylic	M	G	E	E	E
12. Polyester on asbestos/metal composite					
Min 100 μm film oil-free polyester	G	G	G	G	E

Note: E excellent, G good, M moderate, P poor.

Table 4.1 cont.

| Surface finish on aluminium | Type of enviroment | | | | | |
| | External | | | Internal | | |
	Coastal	Industrial and urban	Suburban and rural	Wet and possibly polluted	Dry and unpolluted	Inaccessible enclosed in dry cavity
1. Solution vinyl Min 20 μm vinyl chloride acetate copolymer	S	S	L	M	VL	VL
2. Alkyds Min 20 μm alkyd and oil-free polyester	L	L	L	M	VL	VL
3. Acrylics Min 20 μm thermosetting and thermoplastic acrylic copolymers	L	L	L	M	VL	VL
4. PVC organosol Min 20 μm siliconised versions of acrylics, alkyds and oil-free polyesters	S*	S	L	M	VL	VL
5. Silicone enamels Min 20 μm siliconised versions of acrylics, alkyds and oil-free polyesters	L	L	L	L	VL	VL
6. Fluoropolymers (liquid applied) Min 20 μm PVF and PVF$_2$	L	L	L	L*	VL	VL
7. Fluoropolymers (film applied) Min 20 μm PVF and PVF$_2$	L	L	L	L*	VL	VL
8. Vinasol Min 75 μm film organic coating PVC homopolymer	–	–	–	–	–	–
9. Plastisol Min 175 μm film organic coating PVC homopolymer liquid-applied	M*	L	L	L*	VL	VL
10. PVC film Min 175 μm film organic coating PVC homopolymer-bonded laminates	M*	L	L	L*	VL	VL
11. Acrylic film Min 50 μm film high molecular weight acrylic	L	L	L	L*	VL	VL
12. Polyester on asbestos/metal composite Min 100 μm film oil-free polyester	–	–	–	–	–	–

Note: Life to first maintenance, S short 2-5 years, M medium 5-10 years, L long 10-20 years, VL vert long 20-50 years, – no information or not applicable. Recommendations for life requirements are based on a relatively high aesthetic standard, especially chalking resistance and colour retention, except in the inaccessible environment. * May be used with caution.

mentioned under item 5 of BS4904, but no tolerances on matching are given for guidance by the specifier on what are the limits of acceptability from one batch of coloured sheet to another. Even a cross-reference to BS 3900 Part D : 1978 *Visual comparison of the colour of paints* would be useful in this respect.

Some manufacturers state permissible deviations in colour change of ΔE to be 1 or less where

$$\Delta E = V\Delta L^2 + \Delta a^2 \Delta b^2$$

This equation expresses mathematically the deviations in colour caused by differences in L (brightness), a (red/green) and b (yellow/blue), the parameters that are used to define colour. The sum of the deviations, E, takes into account the statistical probability that they will not all be at their worst at any one time. Commercially it may be difficult to control all these factors to the same extent and, for example, the b factor could be a consistent variable and still allow E to be within the rule.

Finishes for metal sheeting

Sheet steel

Profiled steel sheet is available with a variety of finishes. The principal types for cladding are as follows.

Hot-dipped galvanizing

This is a zinc finish, which may be spangled or matt.

Hot-dipped zinc/aluminized steel

This is a coating (aluminium finish) consisting of an alloy of approximately 55% aluminium/45% zinc, normally sold as Galvalume, Zincalume or Aluzinc. It is slightly more expensive than galvanizing, but offers better corrosion resistance.

Polyvinyl chloride on hot-dipped galvanizing

PVC Organasol is no longer in widespread use, and the most common finish is PVC Plastisol, which can be liquid applied or used as a bonded laminate. The surface will invariably be textured or embossed. This can be considered as a 'thick' coating material with typical nominal thickness of 200 μm.

Acrylic or silicone enamels on hot-dipped galvanizing

Typically 20 μm with a smooth texture, this offers a different colour range from PVC. Siliconized versions of acrylics are also available, and modified silicone and acrylic finishes are now being used, particularly in the USA, as thin 'premium' coatings.

Fluoropolymers on hot-dipped galvanizing

Polyvinylidene fluorides, PVF and PVF_2, are also in widespread use as thin coatings (typically 20 μm), which offer good resistance to weathering. They are usually a mixture of PVF_2 and acrylic and their performance will depend on the particular formulation applied.

Acrylic-modified polyester resin over bitumen/asbestos bonded to steel

This is a very thick coating (overall thickness 555 μm), which is heavily textured, e.g. Galbestos (not now available).

Acrylic-modified polyester on an epoxy base

This is a very 'thick' coating offering good weathering characteristics (e.g. H. H. Robertson's Versacor).

The thicker PVC coatings (Plastisol) offer a better resistance to wear and abrasion than the thinner fluoropolymers (PVF_2) and silicone enamels; however, the PVC colours are not so stable, and tend to fade in ultraviolet light. A general rule might be to use PVC in areas where surface wear might be expected, e.g. roofs, and to use the fluoropolymers where colour integrity is important for reasons of appearance, e.g. walls.

In order to prevent discoloration and deterioration of the organic paint finish, particularly with PVC coatings, it is important that the temperature in use should not exceed the safe temperature ranges of the finishes used (Fig. 4.19). Typical safe temperature ranges for different coatings are:

PVC (inc. Plastisol)	50°C to 79°C
acrylics	50°C to 100°C
fluoropolymers (inc. PVF$_2$)	50°C to 120°C
acrylic polyester	50°C to 70°C

Sheets of dark colour, such as chocolate brown, cause the most problems in heat build-up, particularly those with an insulation layer immediately behind the sheet. In general, black and dark colours can be expected to reach temperatures of 80°C during summer conditions, medium colours 65°C and white or bright aluminium 50°C.

At the Second International Conference on the Durability of Building Materials and Components at

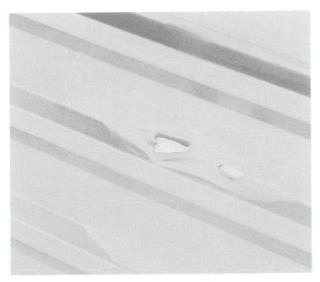

Fig. 4.19 Delamination of outer paint finish due to safe temperatures being exceeded.

Washington, USA, 1981, D. A. Thomas explained that it was generally recognized that organic coatings are permeable to water and oxygen, and also to ions, so even a defect-free coating could not be expected to give permanent protection in sufficiently active environments (Thomas, 1981). Thus the quality of the primer coating is critical to the durability of the paint finish. At the same conference, C. Christ showed the results of tests carried out on two paint systems: an acrylic and a modified fluoropolymer with various types of zinc and aluminium substrates (Christ, 1981). The aluminium-coated substrate was rated better than all other painted substrates at three or four exposure sites. The thickness and weight of the primer are also critical. BS 3083 : 1959 defines the types of zinc coatings and tolerances on the sizes of sheets for determining the weight of zinc. In general, sheeting with the heavier zinc or aluminium coatings beneath the paint films will suffer from less overall deterioration than those with lighter metallic coating weights.

Aluminium

The aluminium industry has always insisted that its material does not need painting, as it has its own built-in protective surface coating of aluminium oxide, which forms immediately on exposure to the atmosphere. However, in order to compete with the colours of paint finishes available for steel cladding, manufacturers have produced a number of organic-coated colour finishes for aluminium sheets. Colour anodizing is limited in that it only really offers black, grey, gold or bronze finishes.

Thus profiled aluminium sheet is available with mill finish, anodized, or with an organic coating. Mill finish is a natural oxidized surface, which darkens with age. Anodized finishes are generally about 25 μm thick according to BS 3987 : 1964 and BS 1615 : 1972. There are five different methods of colour anodizing:

organic dyes, which do not penetrate deeply into the anodic film and are therefore vulnerable to abrasion; many of these are as light fast as inorganic pigments, but some start to fade within two years;

— inorganic pigments, which are used for gold and bronze finishes;

— electrolytic colour, which is deposited deeper than organic dyes to produce black, bronze and grey finishes that resist ultraviolet radiation and abrasion;

— integral or hard colour, where organic acids produce results similar to the electrolytic process;

— special alloys, which produce a grey or gold finish during anodizing.

Aluminium sheeting can be either supplied as precoated fluoropolymers or post-coated as alkyd finish.

The important thing to realize is that the stoved-on alkyd finish has to be applied after forming. Because PVF_2 and acrylics are precoated, they are supplied to the fabricator as finished sheets for forming. Alkyd finishes have to be stoved on after forming.

The safe temperature range for aluminium is $-80\,°C$ to $+100\,°C$, above which gradual loss of strength occurs. Above these temperature ranges the colour coating will also discolour and deteriorate. Some colours reflect or absorb heat more than others, and dark colours are more likely to reach much higher surface temperatures than light colours. It is important to obtain assurances from the manufacturer on the relative durability, colour fastness and temperature limitations of the various colours available.

For both aluminium and steel profiled sheeting, colour matching between batches of sheet and flashings is often a problem. Samples of the limits of colour change can be approved before ordering, but some mismatch of colours on a large job is inevitable. The

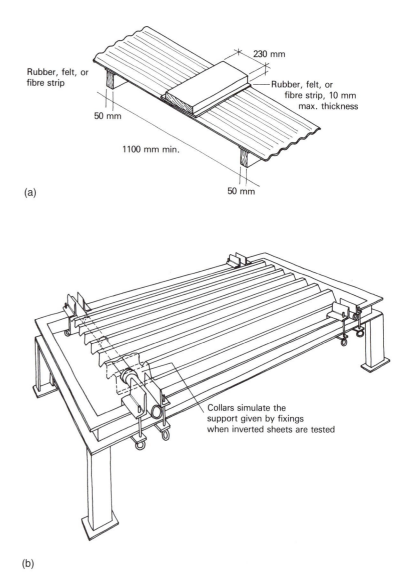

Fig. 4.20 Test rigs for measurement of the strength of metal profiled sheeting (courtesy of British Standards Institution: (a) based on Fig. 6 of BS 4624 : 1981, and (b) based on Fig. 2 of BS 5427 : 1976, with permission).

selection of neutral colours for sheeting or contrasting colours for flashings is a way of overcoming this difficulty.

Performance criteria

The acoustic, thermal, strength, and fire behaviour criteria are compared for steel and aluminium in Table 4.2. In general, the mean value for airborne sound reduction through profiled sheeting is not better than 28 dB unless additional insulation is provided with a back-up construction of mineral wool, in which case it is possible to achieve 36 dB. With such a construction, U-values of 1.8 W/m^2 °C are normally possible (Table 4.3).

In considering strength, steel and aluminium profiled sheeting can be designed to withstand a deflection of span/90 (span dimension divided by 90; Fig. 4.20). Because the performance of cladding is often determined by the deflection criterion, the limit chosen is important. Most manufacturers now consider that a limit of span/90 does not represent good roofing practice, and is likely to lead to troubles from leaks developing at laps. Thus moves are being made to introduce more stringent controls for roof sheeting. Test rigs for the measurement of the strength of metal profiled sheeting are included in BS 5427. A comprehensive description of performance criteria for wall and roof cladding is given in the CEGB guide (CEGB, 1970), which includes sections on loading and strength, fire rating, thermal insulation and acoustic properties.

Resistance to hard body impact is another important characteristic of metal cladding systems, and manufacturers should be asked for results of impact tests (Fig. 4.21).

Installation

Most manufacturers include guidance in their trade literature on the method of handling and storage of their

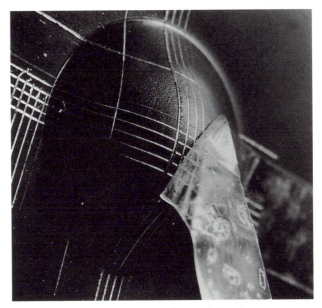

Fig. 4.21 Hard body impact test for steel sheeting,

material on site. All the manufacturers of profiled metal depend upon nominated subcontractors for the detailed design and erection of their cladding. The quality of workmanship on site, particularly at the edge of sheets and the method of fixing, are important factors in the proper assembly of profiled sheeting. Edges of sheets crumpled in handling can look unsightly. The present vogue of using profiled metal horizontally (Fig. 4.12) imposes an even greater requirement for care in the assembly and fixing of flashings and trims.

One of the advantages of profiled sheet metal cladding is that, with care, the fixing subcontractors can adjust the setting out of their sheets to take account of inaccuracies in the structural framing. Fixers prefer to pull on rather than bend sheets to fit an overall dimension, and thus the mean size of the sheets in manufacture is normally below the target size.

Although sheet cladding is subject to very close dimensional control during manufacture, the designer

Table 4.2 Relative performance of steel and aluminium cladding

	Steel	Aluminium
Acoustic	A mean value for airborne sound reduction through 1.6 mm mild steel sheet is 28 dB. Additional insulation can be provided by a back-up construction. An insulated cladding, such as 9 mm plasterboard, 25 mm mineral wool and profiled steel sheet has a mean sound index of 36 dB. The same construction without mineral wool has 30.9 dB reduction. A steel lining tray with 12.5 mm urethane in place of plasterboard and mineral wool insulation and foam sealing strips offer 32.9 dB.	A mean value for airborne sound reduction through 1.6 mm aluminium sheet is 18 dB.
Thermal	The conductivity (k) for carbon steel is 50 W/m °C. Typical U-values for steel sheeting given in Table 4.4.	The conductivity (k) for a typical aluminium alloy is 160 W/m °C. To calculate thermal transmittance (U) see BRE Digest 108 Standard U-values. Aluminium foil increases insulation only if it faces a cavity.
Strength	Figures published in manufacturers' trade literature are not necessarily comparable. Plannja, for example, use high tensile steel for their profiles which increases the permissible span across supports, BSC in describing the properties of their profile make reference to BS 2989: 1975. Manufacturers should be asked to explain the basis of their calculations. BS 5427 permits deflections of span/90.	The tensile strength of the two main aluminium alloys used in the UK is: BS 1470-Ns 3-1 175 N/mm^2; BS 4300/6-NS31-H6, 185 N/mm^2 (BS 4868). Thin aluminium may damage easily on-site, particularly from ladders or equipment.
Behaviour in fire	Profiled steel cladding has no fire resistance as defined in BS 476 : Part 8. Where fire resistance is required, steel sheet can be suitable fire-resisting lining. Profiled steel sheet is classified as 'not easily ignitable' (p) to BS 476 Part 5 and 'non-combustible' to BS 476 Part 4. Profiled steel sheet without a finish can be graded as Class 0 surface spread of flame classification. For classification of sheets with proprietary coatings, the manufacturer should be consulted and if required a test certificate obtained.	Profiled aluminium sheet cladding has no fire resistance as defined in BS 476 : Part 8. It is classified as 'not easily ignitable' (p) to BS 476 Part 5 and 'not combustible' to BS 476 Part 4. Aluminium sheeting with mill finish can be graded as Class 0 spread of flame. For classification of sheets with a proprietary coating it would be necessary to obtain a test certificate from the manufacturer concerned. Obviously it can be used as a total fire-resistant construction with a suitable back-up material.

Table 4.3 Thermal performance - typical U-values

Material	Construction	U-value (W/m² °C)
Steel	1. Plastic-covered steel sheet	5.7
	2. As 1, but with cavity and aluminium foil-backed plasterboard lining	1.9
Aluminium	1. Bright surface inside and outside	2.6
	2. Dull surface outside, bright surface inside	2.8
	3. As 1, but with cavity and aluminium foil-backed plasterboard lining	1.8
	4. As 2, but with cavity and aluminium foil-backed plasterboard lining	2.6

cannot assume that no tolerances are necessary, as spreading of sheets can cause cutting or use of infill pieces on corners and junctions. Fixing contractors need guidance from the designers on where tolerances have been allowed for in the design.

One method of controlling the setting out of profiled sheeting is to use setting-out or spacer jigs mounted on the supporting framework.

The minimum height of stacking profiled sheets on site can be important in reducing the effect of spreading of the overall width of those sheets at the bottom of the stack. Even the way in which the units are lifted on and off the lorry can affect the dimension if they are not crated correctly.

Effect of temperature change on fixings

The external surface of aluminium sheeting will have to withstand a maximum daily temperature range of 50 °C if mill finish or light coloured, and up to 70 °C if dark coloured. As the coefficient of linear expansion of aluminium is 23×10^{-6} °C, these temperature ranges mean that an 8 m long sheet will expand about 10 mm and 13 mm for light- and dark-coloured sheets respec-

tively. It is necessary to accommodate this movement on dark-coloured sheets by oversize holes or non-rigid fixings, but no special requirements are necessary for light-coloured or mill finish sheets. For sheets over 8 m in length, non-rigid fixings should always be used. There is no need to provide expansion joints across the width of the sheet, because the profile will accommodate movement. For steel sheets, the coefficient of linear expansion of steel is 12×10^{-6} °C, which means that an 8 m long sheet will expand 5–7 mm. The inherent flexibility of the material can accommodate this, but over 8 m non-rigid fixings should be used.

Position of fixings

Using metal sinusoidal sheeting, primary fixing should be made through the crown of the corrugations. However, using trapezoidal metal sheeting, fixing in the crown of the profiles can cause spreading of the sheets and damage to the metal, and thus it is normally advisable to fix in the troughs (Fig. 4.22). Maximum fixing centres are 450 mm or every third corrugation, whichever is the less.

Secondary fixings secure one sheet to another so as to exclude wind and rain and provide continuity from sheet to sheet for the dispersion of applied loads. For wall claddings the shear strength of fixings in the centre of the crown is usually adequate, provided that they are no further than 500 mm apart. In some cases it may be possible to provide secret fixings at the side laps between sheets (Fig. 4.23).

Types of fixing

Primary fixings attaching metal cladding to steel rails are commonly self-tapping screws (Fig. 4.24).

Blind light rivets are usually used for secondary fixings in metal claddings. For steel sheeting, cadmium-plated Monel metal rivets should be used, not cadmium-plated mild steel. Rivets in aluminium sheeting should be aluminium alloy (Fig. 4.25).

Cartridge-assisted fasteners, as shown in Fig. 4.26, are used to secure metal roof deck units, but are not used where watertightness relies upon careful tightening against a washer seal, such as is required when fixing roof and wall cladding sheets. Welded or screwed stud fixings for impaled sheets should not be used for metal sheet cladding.

For the aluminium roof sheeting at Stansted Airport the sheeting was fixed to the supporting steelwork on the ground. Because of the improved quality control available with visual inspection at ground level,

fixing through the trough of profiles was possible (Fig. 4.27).

Sheet cladding may fail at the fixings, either by pull-through or by failure of the fixing itself. Fixing should therefore be specified to include nuts, washers and weather-seal devices, all preferably from the same manufacturer.

Compatibility with other materials

Compatibility with other materials is also an important consideration, particularly when using aluminium.

Fig. 4.22 Fixing positions using steel or aluminium sheets: (a) crown fixings for sinusoidal sheeting; (b) trough fixings for trapezoidal sheeting.

Fig. 4.23 Examples of side-lap joints with secret fixings: (a) fixings without accessory section; (b) fixing with accessory section.

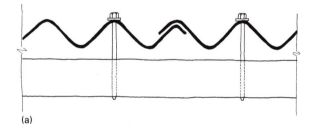

(a)

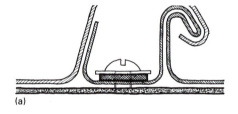

(a)

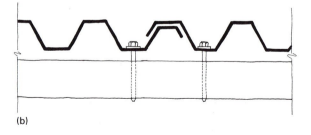

(b)

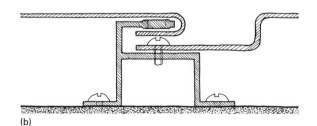

(b)

Aluminium is particularly susceptible to electrolytic corrosion with dissimilar materials. With an organic coating, it is liable to attack if pierced or cut, and anodized aluminium is as susceptible as the untreated metal. There is no corrosive action between aluminium and zinc or between zinc coatings and galvanizing.

Aluminium sheeting, whether organically coated or not, suffers attack from many building materials. Direct contact should be avoided by good detailing and efficient drainage to prevent water run-off. If unavoid-

able, the protective measures listed in Table 4.4 can be taken.

Hot-dip zinc-coated steel suffers moderate attack from copper alloys, iron, steel, some timbers, cement, concrete, plaster, asbestos cement, copper-bearing paints and stainless steel, particularly if water run-off from material onto this cladding occurs. Direct contact should be avoided by good detailing, and efficient drainage will prevent run-off.

Organic coatings on hot-dip zinc-coated steel are unaffected by all common building materials, unless

Fig. 4.24 Examples of self-tapping screws: (a) 12 point plastic head type 'Z' cone-pointed screw with sealing ring to BS 1494 Part 1 Fig. 17; (b) modified version of (a) with load-spreading head; (c) modified version of (b) with spacing collar; (d) self-drilling screw.

Fig. 4.25 Rivets for secondary fixings in metal cladding: (a) pop rivet; (b) sealed-end rivet.

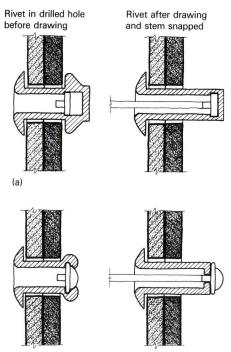

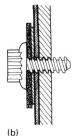

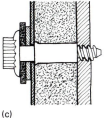

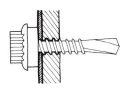

(a)　　　(c)

(b)　　　(d)

Table 4.4 Protective measures for aluminium sheeting

Copper alloys	No protective measure possible; avoid direct contact and water run-off from copper onto aluminium, unless organically coated.
Iron and steel	*Direct contact.* Unless organically coated, use non-aggressive protective paint, e.g. zinc chromate. Avoid copper-bearing paints. In industrial and marine atmospheres, use non-rotting chromate insulating tape. *Water run-off.* Paint iron, galvanize and paint steel (non-copper-bearing, non-aggressive paint).
Lead	Unless organically coated, avoid contact and run-off.
Timber	Compatible non-copper-based preservative (see CP 1430) bituminous paint or felt or building paper.
Boards	Moisture barrier, such as building paper or polythene.
Concrete, plaster, asbestos cement	Bituminous paint and felt insert between contact surfaces.

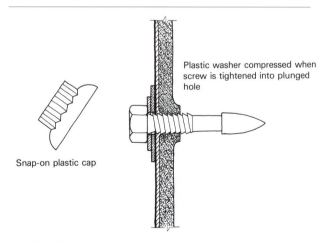

Snap-on plastic cap

Plastic washer compressed when screw is tightened into plunged hole

Fig. 4.26 Cartridge fasteners for metal cladding.

Fig. 4.27 Aluminium roof sheeting at Stansted Airport, fixed on the ground and lifted into position as complete assembly.

they are cut or pierced, when they behave similarly to hot-dip zinc-coated sheet.

Joints between sheets

Side laps of one corrugation will generally prevent driving rain passing through the outer cladding, but when exposure is 'severe' (e.g. in areas with a driving rain index of 7 or more) an increased lap may be needed (Fig. 4.28).

Side laps may sometimes need to be increased locally to avoid cutting sheets at corners and openings. Such laps are easy to increase with regular profiles, but are difficult with irregular profiles and sheets with bonded insulation.

End-lap joints on walls will normally be 100 mm, and on roofs 150 mm, but when exposure is severe the end-lap should be increased to 200 mm.

Sealing of lap joints with mastic is generally not used in vertical sheeting for weather protection. However, sealed side-laps are required for pitched roof-cladding below 15° pitch (Falconer, 1981). Swedish building practice HusAMA also recommends weather seals for profiled sheet roofing for pitches below 14°, and requires side-laps to be joined with screws with washers to protect from leakage, or rivets maximum centre-to-centre 500 mm. Corner details are an important design consideration. Figure 4.29 shows various ways of turning a corner using flashings. Over-sheet corner flashings usually need to be wide in relation to the profile of the main cladding and tend to conflict with it in scale. Appearance and weathering are improved by inverting the edges of the angle, but this allows little flexibility in positioning the sheets with the profile shown. Curved-over-sheet corner flashings can also be used.

Using over- and under-sheet corner flashings, these can be shaped to match the profile of the main cladding. The upturned lip of the main cladding is also covered, offering a better water check.

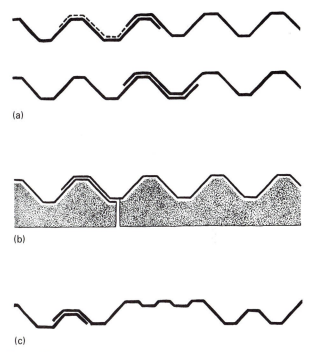

(a)

(b)

(c)

Fig. 4.28 Side-laps between sheets. (a) Maximum flexibility in side-laps is provided by sheets with uniform troughs and half-corrugations. (b) Standard sheets with factory-bonded backings do not permit variations in side-lap. (c) Sheets in which corrugations are not uniform do not allow variations in side lap.

With under-sheet flashings, in order to avoid the exposure of an upturned lip, one of the cladding sheets has to be reversed. The length of the under-leg of the flashing offers some tolerance in the assembly. In some cases the sheets are butted against the steel frame and the frame exposed at the corner (Fig. 4.30).

With horizontal cladding, various corner-joint details have been used including welded corners and special GRP closer ends with matching finish, as used at IBM Greenford (architects: Foster Associates). Tolerances in manufacture and assembly are even more critical with horizontal cladding, because any misalignment of the profiles can cause apparent waving. Slip trays can also be used at the joints between horizontal cladding; however, it is sometimes difficult to match the profiles exactly, and the thickness of the slip tray

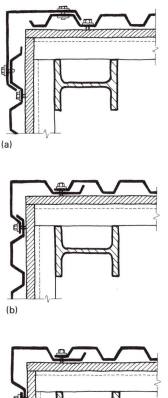

(a)

(b)

(c)

Fig. 4.29 Various methods of corner detailing using flashings: (a) over-sheet corner flashing; (b) over- and under-sheet corner flashing; (c) under-sheet corner flashing.

tends to make the edge of the sheet more obvious in appearance.

Profiled sheeting is best used in well-proportioned large areas, to enclose the main structure with the minimum of joints with other materials. Translucent sheets are available to match most profiles. If opening lights or transparent areas are required, sheets of patent glazing are better than small isolated windows, because they relate more naturally to the scale of the main cladding and reduce the problem of jointing around window openings.

Butt-end joints between sheeting and windows are normally made with Z-flashings or propriety neoprene sections (Fig. 4.31).

Sheeting rails and liner trays

The optimum use of sheeting rails to support profiled cladding is critical to the economic use of the material and its capacity to withstand wind loading. Constrado (1980) shows typical spans of around 2 m for profiled steel cladding, depending upon its profile. Thus sheeting rails are required at intervals up the height of the wall to support the cladding. These sheeting rails must themselves be designed to span between the main support columns (Fig. 4.32).

As an alternative to sheeting rails, liner trays can be used, which when clipped together (Fig. 4.33) act as horizontal rails at 500 mm intervals. The interaction of cladding and liner trays provides a composite lattice effect. Mineral fibre insulation can be pushed into the liner trays from the outside before the outer profile cladding is fixed. The flat surface of the liner tray, which can be prepainted, then acts as a finished inner lining to the construction. The liner can either be used horizontally as described above, or vertically, used in conjunction with horizontal profiled cladding.

Fig. 4.30 Corner detail with exposed steel frame.

Fig. 4.32 Sheeting rails are needed to span between main supports.

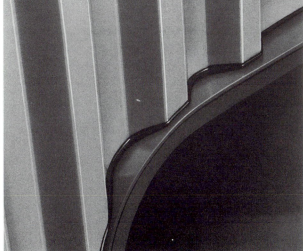

Fig. 4.31 Neoprene flashing at window opening.

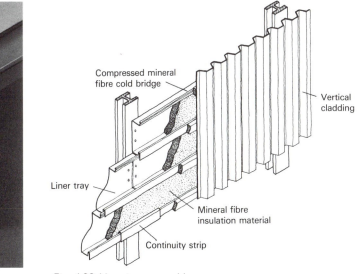

Compressed mineral fibre cold bridge

Vertical cladding

Liner tray

Mineral fibre insulation material

Continuity strip

Fig. 4.33 Liner tray assembly.

References and further reading

Brookes A. J. (1980) Claddings 1 – Product selection and speci-fiaction of profiled asbestos cement, steel and aluminium sheets. *Architects' Journal*, **172** (41), 705–719.

BSI (1976) BS 5427 : 1976, *Code of practice for performance and loading criteria for profiled sheeting in building*, British Standards Institution, London.

CEGB (1970) *Design memorandum – wall and roof cladding*, 097/117 issue, 12 April, Central Electricity Generating Board, London.

Christ, C. (1981) Outdoor durability and performance of pre-painted, cold rolled galvanized and aluminized steels, in *Proceedings of International Conference on the Durability of Building Materials and Components*, 14–16 September, National Bureau of Standards, Gaithersburg, USA, pp. 313–326.

Constrado (1980) *Profiled Steel Cladding and Decking for Commercial and Industrial Buildings*, Doc SMP/38/80, Constrado, London.

Falconer, P. (1981) Industrial pitched roofs – the art of con-struction series. *Architects' Journal*, **174** (41), 759–773.

MacGregor, I. (1981) *Coil coating*. Build, No. 29, October, Build-ing Research Association of New Zealand.

Metal Roof Deck Association (1970) *Code of Design and Tech-nical Requirements for 'Light' Gauge Metal Roof Decks*, Metal Roof Deck Association, Sussex.

Property Services Agency, Method of Building Group (1979) *Technical Guidance – Sheet Cladding – Non-loadbearing Profiled Asbestos Cement, Steel and Aluminium.*

Thomas, D. A. (1981) Initial degradation of corrosion protec-tion by organic coatings, in *Proceedings of International Con-ference on the Durability of Building Materials and Components*, 14–16 September, National Bureau of Stan-dards, Gaithersburg, USA, pp. 297–303.

5

Sheet metal, composite metal panels and rain screens

The idea is to create a flexible framework, a framework which embraces the floor, the walls and the ceiling so that within that framework the plan is completely changeable.

Norman Foster (1978)

Introduction

In architecture the father of pressed metal panel systems, *le panneau*, is undoubtedly Jean Prouvé. Many such panel systems were developed by Prouvé including his early use of metal composite panels at the Aero Club Roland Garros in 1935 and the façade designed for Cours Conception Construction, an industrialized school building system designed in 1963 (Huber and Steinegger, 1971).

In the 1950s the stainless steel clad Airstream Caravan (Fig. 5.1) became a twentieth century icon of prefabrication. Prefabrication predominantly takes two structural forms: **monocoque shells** and **framed construction**. Renzo Piano's design for the Fiat VSS experimental vehicle (Fig. 5.2) showed the application of a structural frame and clip-on plastic cladding to car manufacture. Most composite cladding systems in building have been developed for use as spanning between framed construction.

Early examples of metal cladding systems, mainly in the USA and France, usually consisted of metal undersill panels mounted into curtain walling assemblies known in the USA as 'stick' systems, or in France

Fig. 5.1 Airstream caravan.

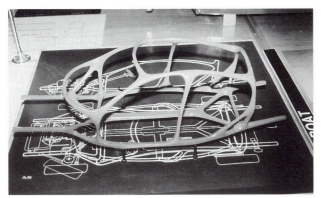

Fig. 5.2 Fiat car by Renzo Piano.

as *la grille*. In this way a continuous curtain wall could be used, with the metal, solid (non-glazed) panels masking the floors and columns. Such infill panels were often small in size (typically 1.75 m long × 0.75 m high), and were often pressed into a decorative or embossed profile. During the 1950s such systems were in widespread use in multi-storey buildings, typified by the rigid chequer-pattern façades produced by the exposed curtain walling framework (Fig. 5.3).

Aesthetic objections to this form of facade, together with improved legislation on energy conservation and insulation, encouraged architects to consider complete panel assemblies, in which the solid, insulation and opening elements are fabricated on sub-frames in the factory and transported to the site and erected as one unit.

There are essentially four types of sheet metal and composite panel system (Fig. 5.4):

- rolled flat sheet panels mounted onto a supporting framework;
- box-type panels (including proprietary panels), usually with foamed cores;
- laminated panels;
- rain screen panels.

The second and third types can be considered as composite metal panels.

Composite metal panels

A combination of predictable thermal and structural performance quickly led architects to see the benefits of using composite metal panels. Composite construction is the bonding together of layers of materials to form a rigid structure. The Mosquito bomber (Fig. 5.5) was an early example of composite construction in aircraft design. Composite construction is now extensively used

Fig. 5.3 Typical metal cladding system in the USA.

in products as diverse as tennis rackets and jet aircraft. The principal form of composite construction is two thin sheets held apart by a lightweight core to which they are bonded. It is the spacing of the two sheets that is mainly responsible for the rigidity of the final composite: the wider the spacing, the greater the spanning capabilities of the finished product. Early developments of composite steel panels in the UK included the panels for the Oxford Regional Hospital Board System, 1963–73. A gasket joint designed by Jan Silva was based on a jointing principle developed by Jean Prouvé in which a neoprene gasket fixed to a steel channel is compressed against the panel profile by bolts at intervals up the height of the panel (Fig. 5.6).

Some difficulties were experienced in the foaming of the polyurethane insulation of these panels and in ensuring the integrity of the skins and the core material. The panel system was later abandoned in favour of a more conventional horizontal profiled high-tensile steel cladding with site-applied insulation.

The economics of using metal composite units depend upon standardization of unit sizes, and it is perhaps not surprising that their use tends to be associated with a system of coordinated dimensions. For example, during the 1970s, development in open system tendering by local authority consortia schools programmes, such as the South Eastern Architects Consortium (SEAC Mark 4), encouraged the production of pressed metal panels mounted within a steel 'third member' subframe. Such panels were manufactured by Gordon Durham Aycliffe Ltd as Conatus panels, and by Brockhouse Lightform for SEAC Mark 4. These panels are no longer marketed, probably because they proved to be too expensive in comparison with other cladding materials when used for the variety of panel sizes required for school buildings.

The use of proprietary composite panels for industrial buildings has been more widespread, where

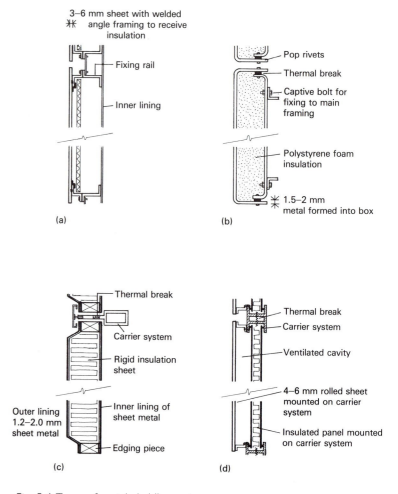

Fig. 5.4 Types of metal cladding system.

standard-width panels are bolted back to a simple structural framework, and where the façade has no, or only a few, windows. Typically a façade unit of this type consists of a profiled sheet, thermal insulation and an internal lining, either produced as a composite unit in the factory or assembled separately on site (Fig. 5.7).

Fig. 5.5 Mosquito bomber.

The Sainsbury Centre (Fig. 5.8) designed by Foster Associates in 1977 was one of the first uses of Superplastic aluminium for insulated composite panels and, more importantly, was one of the first non-commercial, non-industrial buildings to use an interchangeable panel system. Identical 1.8 m × 1.2 m panels were used for both walls and roof, with the weatherproofing joint detail dependent upon the neoprene gasket being mounted back against an aluminium carrier system.

The panels were manufactured by Superform Metals ITC Worcester using vacuum-forming techniques, from a special alloy patented by the British Aluminium Company. This 'supral' alloy has the advantage over conventional aluminium alloy that it will flow or 'run' at the right temperature, and can be extended to ten times its original length. However,

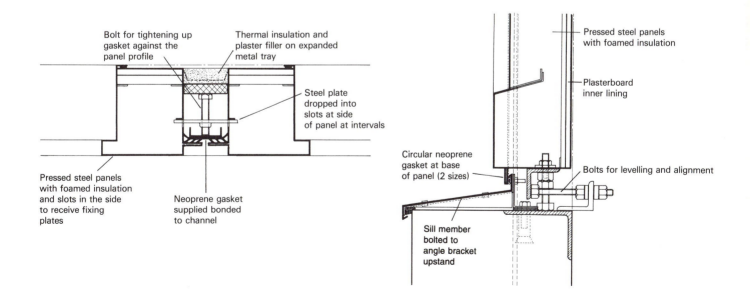

Fig. 5.6 Oxford Regional Hospital Board joint (plan and section).

the process of manufacture is slow and costly, and some technical difficulties were experienced at first in forming the corners of the panels. Each outer tray was filled with 100 mm phenelux foam (curved decorative sections being filled with polystyrene), and the inner skins were then pushed into the outer trays and pop-riveted together through a small section of phenolic foam core, which formed the thermal break at the edge of the panel. Thermal transmission of the panels was U = 0.47 W/m² °C. For a detailed study of this construction see case study 22 in Brookes (1985).

The aim was to produce a U-shaped one-piece continuous ladder gasket, which fitted into an aluminium carrier system by Modern Art Glass, forming not only the main seal but also the guttering system (Fig. 5.9). These neoprene gaskets were manufactured by the Leyland and Birmingham Rubber Company as a lattice framework with two-way joints at mid-points of the overhang vulcanized on site using portable equipment (Fig. 5.10). In this way an interchangeable system of wall and roof panels was achieved. A similar principle of continuous neoprene gaskets was later used at Gatwick Airport North Piers (Fig. 5.11).

The original panels on the Sainsbury Centre failed for a number of reasons and have been replaced by a flat composite panel by H. H. Robertson, which does not have the architectural effect of the original panels, nor is the replaced jointing gasket used in the same consistent way.

Composite panels were also used by Foster at the Renault Centre (Fig. 5.12), where 75 mm thick panels span 4 m between the vertical cladding support. The panel system, which was bolted to the vertical cantilevered columns by three fixings at each end of the panel, provided a very low-cost elevation. A large neoprene skirt takes up the deflection at the top of the assembly (Fig. 5.13). For further details of the construction see case study 21 in Brookes (1985).

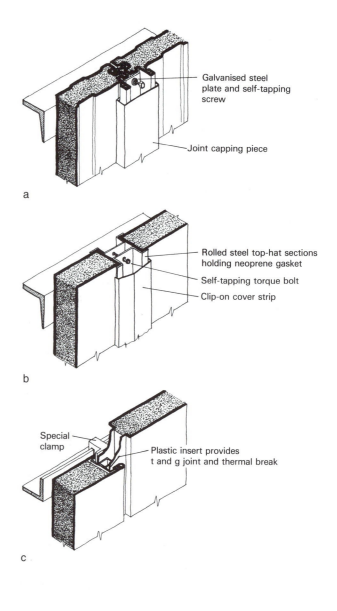

Fig. 5.7 Early examples of proprietary box-type panel joints: (a) Briggs Amasco Perfrisa; (b) Booth-Murie Simplan 1200; (c) Hunter Douglas Luxalon.

Fig. 5.8 Sainsbury Centre panels (architects: Foster Associates).

There are now essentially two types of composite panel. These are:

foamed polyurethane panels:

—   continuous production;
—   batch production;

laminated panels:

—   continuous production;
—   batch production.

Insulation cores

Different types and thickness of sheet material and foam can be used for the insulation cores for composite panels. These are:

—   mineral wool;
—   honeycomb paper core;
—   bead polystyrene rigid sheet;
—   IB polystyrene rigid sheet;
—   polyurethane foam (polyisocyanurate is a modified form of polyurethane to improve fire retardancy).

Polystyrene sheet, which is produced by heating up polystyrene granules and fusing them together with a combination of steam and pressing, is cheaper in material cost than polyurethane foam. However, polyurethane gives better insulation than polystyrene (25 mm thick polyurethane has the same insulation value as 40 mm thick polystyrene; see Fig. 5.14) and it is easier to manufacture. Most manufacturers of box-type proprietary panels prefer to use polyurethane or at least its modified version, polyisocyanurate, which is sometimes used because of its fire retardancy.

The use of any particular type or thickness of core depends upon the stiffness required of the whole

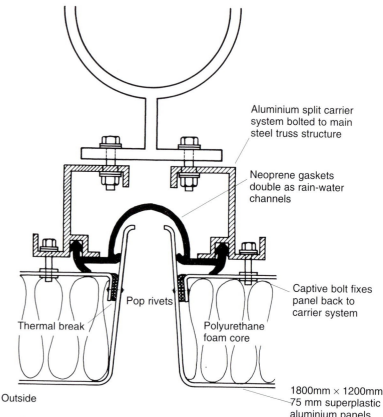

Fig. 5.9 Detail of joint at Sainsbury Centre.

panel and the requirements for thermal and acoustic performance. In general, for foamed materials, the higher the density the stiffer the panel, and the lower the density the better the insulation value. Note that modern foam production is now CFC-free as it no longer uses freon gas as a foaming agent.

Foamed polyurethane panels

The market for foamed polyurethane panels is estimated (1996) as 2.3 million m² in the UK, 7 million m² in Germany and 12 million m² in Italy, of which only a small

Fig. 5.10 Lattice gaskets used at Sainsbury Centre.

Fig. 5.12 Panels at Renault Centre.

Fig. 5.11 Assembly of panels at Gatwick Airport North Piers.

percentage, say 5%, are made by batch production using vertical or horizontal foaming. The majority are made on continuous foaming lamination lines by such companies as Hoesch (Germany), Elcom (Italy), Forges D'Haironville (France), Kingspan (UK) and Perfrisa (Spain).

Polyurethane and polyisocyanurate foams can be foamed in place during the production, by:

- continuous foaming;
- vertical pouring; or
- horizontal pouring.

Becker (1968) gives more details of methods of in-place foam production and other detailed considerations for sandwich panel design. Profiled sheets of

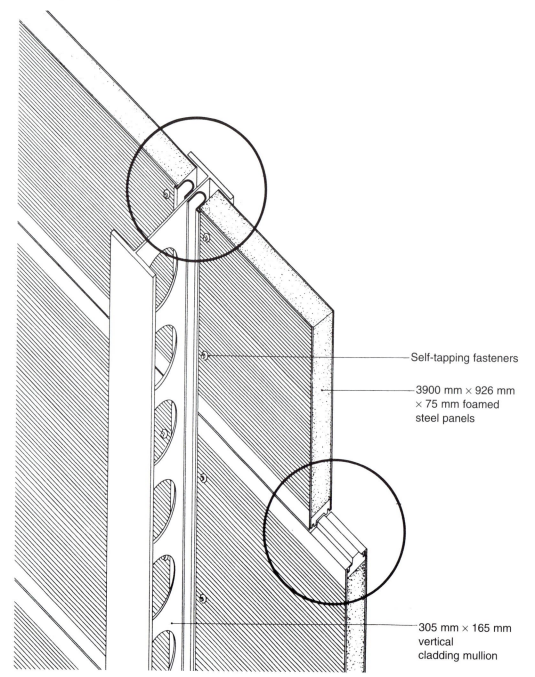

Self-tapping fasteners

3900 mm × 926 mm
× 75 mm foamed
steel panels

305 mm × 165 mm
vertical
cladding mullion

Fig. 5.13 Detail of panel at Renault Centre.

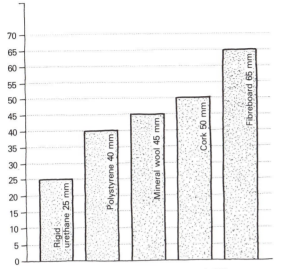

Fig. 5.14 Relative insulation performance of different core materials.

Fig. 5.15 Typical continuous foaming line.

metal with polyisocyanurate backing are often produced on a continuous process (Fig. 5.15). Surfactants are necessary to ensure a closed cell and to maintain the quality of the foam (Fig. 5.16).

Although well-insulated buildings help to reduce energy consumption, and indirectly limit carbon dioxide emissions by decreasing the amount of heating they require, increasing concern over the potential effects on the ozone layer of CFC gases used as foaming agents has led to a review of the materials and their manufacturing processes, resulting in the Montreal Protocol. Now producers of foamed polyurethane offer foaming formulations containing blowing agents such as HCFC141b. Early use of carbon dioxide blowing agents to reduce the effects of CFCs caused problems due to temperature variations on flat panels. It was also more difficult to use carbon dioxide blowing agents with polyisocyanurate foams, which had been introduced for their improved fire resistance.

Development work is still continuing on new foam formulations to improve the efficiency of the manufacturing process. One difficulty for the manufacturers of foamed panels in changing the foaming agents used is that these modifications can result in slower production rates and a slight reduction in thermal performance. In theory, panels with modified foamed cores would need to be thicker and therefore potentially more expensive. Inherent in the manufacture of continuous foamed panels is the need to control density to maintain compressive strength. In laminating sheet core materials, it is the adhesion between the core materials and the skins that gives the panel its strength. The bonding therefore has to be undertaken in conditions of strict quality control. In recent years, manufacturers have understood the importance of good bonding, and they now check the temperature, humidity and coat weight of the adhesive during production

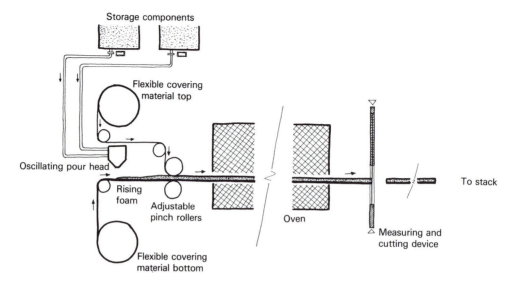

Fig. 5.16 Diagram of continuous foaming process.

as part of their BS 5750 quality management procedures. Following production, checks are made on the strength of the bond to the panel skin, and samples from each production run are tested to destruction.

Foamed panels can also be made by batch production on individual foaming lines (Fig. 5.17), but the most economic production is achieved using a continuously operating line foaming plant. On a continuous horizontal line, which can now produce high-quality panels at a speed of 7 m/s, there is no limit to the length of the panels other than that imposed by the means of transportation and the individual manufacturer's method of fixing and panel configuration. Panels can now be transported on articulated trailers up to 30 m long, and typically panels are 6–12 m long. The width of coils of metal has increased in recent years, so that steel panels can now be produced up to 1300 mm wide and aluminium up to 1500 mm. Foamed panels produced in a vertical-injected foaming press are

normally limited to 600 mm high to control the density of foam over the width of the panel (Fig. 5.18).

Laminated panels

Laminated panels using sheet core materials of extruded or bead polystyrene are increasingly used on more sophisticated 'architectural' buildings. Integrated systems, including composite panels, are supplied complete with doors, windows and louvres. It is noticeable that the divisions are becoming increasingly blurred as the sectors of the market change shape. Manufacturers with previous experience of volume markets are now asked to provide the management expertise to control all stages of the process, including quality control and transportation, and to offer specific guidance on the performance criteria, leading to a more accurate specification for their use within the system market. This process relies on changes in attitudes towards technical specifications and quality control, and a requirement for design input from the manufacturers that may be beyond their present resources. Batch-produced sheet core manufacturers using platten presses (Fig. 5.19) and vacuum presses (Fig. 5.20) concentrate on wall panels only.

Large laminated panels (up to 7 m × 2.5 m) can be pressed together under heat using a platten press, on which a number of panels can be made up from trays, sheet insulation, edging pieces and backing sheets, and stacked together before pressing. Typical of such panels are those produced by Josef Gartner and Co. in Germany, where the outer aluminium sheet is brake pressed and welded into a dish. Into this is placed a honeycomb core with a further aluminium sheet forming the inner lining. The complete assembly is bonded together with a neoprene or timber edging and placed in a large platten press (Fig. 5.19). In this way laminated panels can be produced up to 2.5 m × 7.0 m long.

Vacuum presses (Fig. 5.20) can also be used to press laminated panels, but because the panels are pressed not more than two at a time the production may be slower; producing sandwich panels with either a mineral fibre, polyurethane or honeycomb core up to 1.6 m × 6.0 m long is standard, and larger sizes may be possible after consultation.

Panels can also be laminated using large 'nip' rollers. Using pressing techniques it is possible, with care, to apply a finish prior to fabrication.

Curved panels can be produced, in one direction only, by cold rolling or pressing. Panels curved in three dimensions can be produced by deep-drawing techniques. Curved laminated panels (Fig. 5.21) will inevitably cost more than flat panels, as special forms are required to press the panels, which will increase their cost of production.

Panels using insulation boards have the advantage of batch production, allowing the production of a range of bespoke sizes with variable cores. The laminated cores can include bead polystyrene and extruded

Fig. 5.17 Batch production of foamed panels – horizontal foaming.

Fig. 5.18 Batch production of foamed panels – vertical foaming.

polystyrene, polyurethane, Rockwool Lamella and Foamglass. Bead polystyrene, often used in packaging, does not require a blowing agent, and is available in large size sheets, 1.2 m × 8 m nominally. However, it does have disadvantages: its thermal conductivity (k value 0.034–0.037 W/m K), shrinking immediately after manufacture, and its moisture-permeable open cell structure. Extruded polystyrene has a closed cell structure, is moisture resistant, and of a controlled density with a k value of 0.030–0.035 W/m K. Producers of extruded polystyrene now use HCFCs as foaming agent. These materials contain hydrogen and consequently have a much reduced ODP (ozone depletion potential). Polyurethane, which also has a closed cell structure, uses HCFCs to achieve a k value of 0.025 W/m K.

Mineral wool and honeycomb paper core, which normally contain polystyrene inserts within the core, are used for laminated panel production. The honeycomb core has the advantage that adhesive collects in the holes and offers good adherence to the panel skin. Additional acoustic performance, particularly where improved sound reduction at low frequencies is required, can be obtained by increasing the mass of the panel and laminating asbestos cement sheet and high-density mineral wool into the panel.

The integral strength of the metal and core allows the use of a thinner sheet of between 1.2 and 2.0 mm. Often the outer skin of the panel is brake pressed and shaped prior to being pressed, and the edges of the panel are reinforced with edging pieces of neoprene, or timber, or even foamed glass. It is not unusual for these sandwich panels to be mounted within a steel or aluminium carrier system, using a capping piece and neoprene gasket to support the panel along its four edges.

The process of pressing these thinner sheets and bonding them to the rigid insulation usually provides a

Fig. 5.19 Laminated panel production using platten presses.

Fig. 5.20 Laminated panel production using vacuum presses.

flatter panel than can be produced by rolling the sheet material.

An early use of pressed panels using 64 mm of mineral fibre insulation board sandwiched between two layers of 16 gauge aluminium on 6 mm of asbestos sheet was at the Danish Embassy, London (architects: Arne Jacobsen Dissing and Weitling) (Fig. 5.22).

Laminated sheets can be manufactured as thin infill panelling, 6–10 mm thick, such as Alucobond, manufactured by Swiss Aluminium Ltd, which consists of two sheets of aluminium (Peralumen NS 41), each 0.5 mm thick, bonded to a low-density polyethylene core. The exceptional flatness and stiffness of these thin panels makes them ideal for use with glazing techniques. For example, 2.4 m × 1.25 m panels at Winwick Quay factory, Warrington (architects: Nicholas Grimshaw Partnership) are supported by a 150 mm × 25 mm extruded aluminium presslock system by Modern Art Glass (Fig. 5.23). For a detailed study of this construction see case study 30 in Brookes (1985).

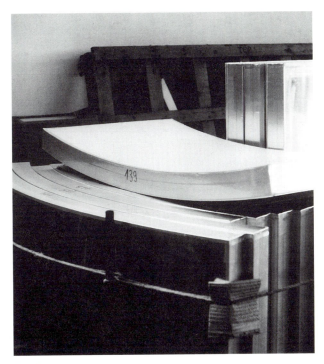

Fig. 5.21 Curved laminated panels.

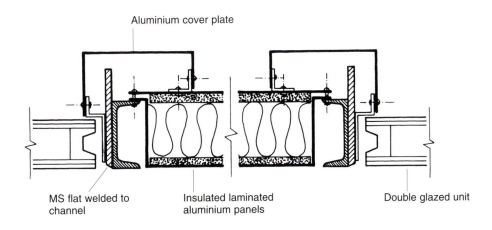

Aluminium cover plate

MS flat welded to channel

Insulated laminated aluminium panels

Double glazed unit

Fig. 5.22 Plan of laminated panel as used at Danish Embassy, London (architects: Arne Jacobsen, Dissing and Weitling).

Alucobond can be curved to a minimum radius of approximately 10 times the panel thickness; typical curves are 30–80 mm radius.

Adhesives

Bearing in mind the need to avoid delamination, the architect should seek advice from the manufacturer on the best type of adhesive related to the possible stresses that may be set up between the laminations, and to the requirements for heat resistance. Lap shear strength up to 28 000 kPa is possible with some adhesives. The relative costs of the different adhesives may not be significant relative to the total cost of the panel.

There are three types of adhesive in widespread use for the production of laminated sandwich panels:

- neoprene contact adhesives;
- one- and two-part polyurethanes;
- one- and two-part epoxies.

It is sometimes difficult to bond mill-finished aluminium or galvanized steel because of the oxide layer on the surface, which must be removed or strengthened chemically. Although special polyurethanes are available, the problem is better solved prior to application of a thin coat of acid etch primer.

Specification

In the consideration of laminated or foamed production there is a perceived benefit by specifiers, particularly for architectural projects, of the refinement of the joint edge. Batch-produced lamination has some advantage in that a formed edge or adaptor can be introduced on all four sides. However, some manufacturers using continuous foam laminating are beginning to introduce formed stop-ends on their production lines.

Specification of composite cladding is normally carried out by architects/engineers for architectural projects and by engineers for cold store applications. For 'special' projects, cladding consultants or façade engineers are increasingly involved. Generally, there is not enough knowledge by specifiers concerning the types of material used, their performance values or characteristics in use. Specifiers complain of manufacturers' technical data being inadequate. Manufacturers complain that specifiers do not give adequate or informed specifications of their requirements. Users and specifiers increasingly recognize the 'fast track' opportunities of using composite cladding, and are seeking greater variation of products, including their jointing and fixing.

Sound performance is not at present a common requirement, but increasingly manufacturers are being asked to respond to specifications requiring higher degrees of sound performance than 25 dB reduction at 100–500 Hz. Fire performance is becoming increasingly a requirement, led by fire insurance requirements and the Loss Prevention Council. Manufacturers, even of continuous foamed panels, are looking at ways of providing cheap fire-performance panels, while maintaining the same compressive strength and thermal performance as currently required. Test evidence is not normally required by specifiers or users, although most manufacturers would supply evidence of load span tables if required.

In the past, manufacturers conscious of this need for quality have obtained BS 5750 Part 2 registration, and have also obtained Agrément Certificates for products. In some cases they have sought continental certification such as Zalussung certification from the German Institut für Bautechnik. However, with the introduction of new CFC-free formulations, many manufacturers have not sought Agrément certification because of the high cost of testing relative to the small demand for this evidence by the specifier.

Part of the procedure necessary to obtain BS

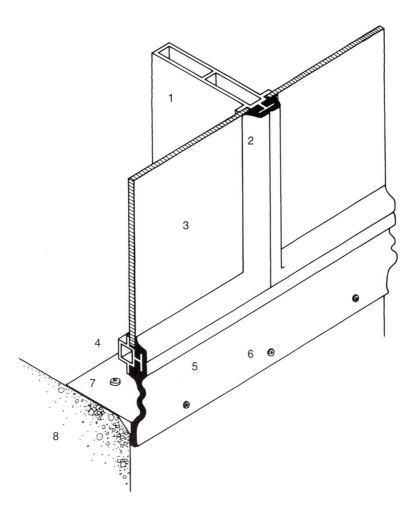

Fig. 5.23 Alucobond sheets at Winwick Quay, Warrington: (1) 150 mm × 25 mm extruded aluminium cladding mullion spanning 4800 mm vertically; (2) preformed continuous neoprene gasket; (3) 6 mm anodic silver finished Alucobond; (4) 25 mm × 25 mm extruded aluminium horizontal cladding rail spanning 1250 mm between mullions; (5) preformed neoprene tolerance strip; (6) self-tapping screws fixing neoprene back aluminium sill; (7) aluminium sill screwed down to concrete slab; (8) 200 mm power-floated reinforced concrete slab.

5750 approval is to show evidence of checking the panels after production, including the bonding of the skins to the cores and the tolerances on size. Typical permissible deviations on dimensions of continuously foamed panels are: length ±4 mm (0–8 mm), thickness ±1 mm, width ±2 mm. Laminated panels, particularly those with PVC-framed edges, can be manufactured to closer degrees of tolerance.

Manufacturers have developed flat panels to meet customer requirements. Curved and cranked shapes are available, allowing freedom of design. However, no panel can be manufactured perfectly flat. Variations are caused partly by the foaming or lamination process. Although it is possible to agree tolerances for flatness, the degrees of visual flatness can be minimized by micro-ribbing or embossing of the panel surface. Some manufacturers of continuously foamed panels claim to improve flatness tolerance to 0.7 mm over 2 m by controlling the stretch of the metal skins.

It is the spacing of the metal sheets that is mainly responsible for the rigidity of the final composite: the wider the spacing, the greater the spacing capabilities of the finished product. Typically, a panel with two skins of 0.6 mm steel and 50 mm of polyurethane insulation can span up to 4 m. A further advantage is that it can be used to combine dissimilar materials. Thus durability, rigidity and insulation can be provided in one product. It is perhaps disappointing therefore that more consideration is not given to the engineering possibilities of selecting density in relation to stiffness and permissible deflection in the same way that suspended glass technology (see Chapter 6) has advanced over recent years.

Delamination

Some composite panels, particularly those with a foamed insulation core, failed in the past because of delamination of the outer skin from the insulation to which they

Fig. 5.24 Typical example of delamination of composite panels.

Fig. 5.25 Stiffening angles to rolled sheet panel.

were bonded (Fig. 5.24). This in turn reduced the spanning characteristics of the panel, because the materials were no longer acting in a composite fashion. Tests carried out at the BRE by Dr R. Thorogood (1979) showed panels that were subject to this phenomenon, and suggested steps to be taken to prevent it. Delamination is caused by the sun heating up the outer skin of the panel, which consequently expands, while the inner skin remains at a low temperature because of the insulation. An unrestrained panel will bow outwards to accommodate this extension, and there will be relatively little stress set up between the outer skin and the core. However, if such a panel is fixed to a structure so that its ability to bow is limited by the fixings, then the stress set up at the interface of the skin and the core will be considerably greater, and delamination is likely to occur. The stresses can be reduced if the edges of the panel are free to bend as the panel bows out and are not restrained by the adjacent panels or the method of fixing.

Other factors in design can reduce the effect of this thermal movement, as follows.

—   Use light colours on the outer skin to reduce the heat gain on the skin.
—   The size of the panel should be taken into consideration. Large panels will deflect more than small ones.
—   Fixings in the centre of panels should be avoided.
—   The adhesive and type of insulation core should be selected to take account of stresses set up by thermal movement.
—   If the inner skin has a higher coefficient of expansion than the outer (i.e. aluminium inner skin/steel outer skin), then the effect of thermal movement will be reduced.

Considerable research has been carried out by reputable manufacturers into the selection of adhesives, insulation cores and specifications of their use. With careful design the issue of delamination can be resolved.

Rolled sheet panels

This type of panel consists of 3–6 mm sheet metal formed into a metal pan on the outside face, either by cutting and welding the metal into a tray or, more usually, by spot-welding angles that form the edge to the tray. The stiffness of the panel thus depends upon the thickness of the metal and the number of stiffening angles (Fig. 5.25).

The panel is supported by a fixing rail or some form of secondary framing, and the insulation is normally applied loosely on site, although in some cases it can be glued to the back of the panel in the factory. The inside face is finished either with another metal sheet or with a conventional interior finish material such as gypsum plasterboard. The essential difference between this type of panel and the other types described is that the insulation and inner linings do not add to the total stiffness of the panel. One problem in manufacturing such panels is that of avoiding the rippling of the surface or 'oil canning effect' and ensuring that the sheet metal is perfectly flat and smooth, which also influences the thickness of the metal used.

In order to allow for thermal expansion of the aluminium rolled sheet, it is now advised that the sheet is not directly connected to the angel framing, but 'floated' onto its supports using Z-section cleats (Fig. 5.26). These cleats are spot-welded to the sheet during fabrication, thus holding it within the frame. Following fabrication, the edges are sealed with a silicone joint. Pins can also be used welded to the back of the sheet onto which the sheets of insulation are mounted.

Many projects in the USA have been constructed using rolled sheet panels. These would include the

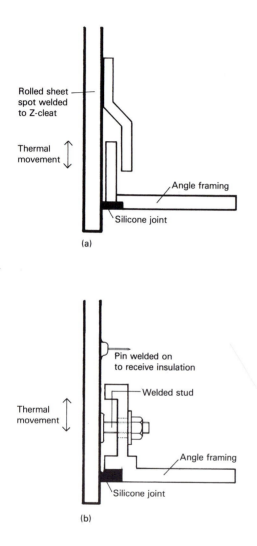

Rolled sheet spot welded to Z-cleat

Thermal movement

Angle framing

Silicone joint

(a)

Pin welded on to receive insulation

Welded stud

Thermal movement

Angle framing

Silicone joint

(b)

Fig. 5.26 Alternative methods of fixing angle framing to rolled steel panels: (a) Z-section cleat spot-welded to sheet; (b) welded stud on outer sheet with slotted holes in angle framing.

City-Corp Building in New York (curtain walling by Flour City) and the Richard J. Hughes Justice Complex at Trenton, NJ (architects: the Hillier Group, Princeton), also supplied and erected by Flour City. Such panels were also used at the Federal Reserve Bank building in Boston (Fig. 5.27) (architect: Hugh Stubbins), where flanges were welded onto 5 mm plate aluminium, and the Bronx Centre, New York (architect: Richard Meier), where 3 mm aluminium sheet was brake pressed and the corners formed by cutting and welding into a tray. These were mounted onto a secondary framing on site, with insulation and inner linings applied *in situ*. For a detailed description of these projects, see Murphy (1978).

The maximum size of rolled sheet panels tends to relate to the size of sheets available (normally 1.5 mm width maximum), and the weight of units when assembled. Panels at the Bronx Centre, which were mainly 3.45 m wide × 0.75 m, 1.5 m and 1.35 m high, made near-maximum use of available rolled sheet sizes. Some curved panels were also used on the projecting staircase enclosures, 3.6 m high × 0.862 m wide (Fig. 5.28). Because of cost, plasterboard linings were selected for this project, and it is interesting to note that the curved corners to the windows had to be made good in plaster on the inside face. Figure 5.29 shows detail from the Johnson & Johnson building, which incorporates a gutter system at the base of the panels to collect any water that may penetrate the sealant (usually silicone) joint system. Weepholes are also provided to discharge the water to the outside face. Also note the method of 'floating' the aluminium sheet onto the panel framework, using studs welded onto the sheet with slotted holes to permit thermal movement.

European examples of rolled sheet panel construction would include the Hochhaus Dresdner Bank in Frankfurt (panels by Josef Gartner; architects: Becker,

Fig. 5.27 Federal Reserve Bank, Boston (architect: Hugh Stubbins).

Becker and Partners). Here the panels consist of 2.5 mm aluminium rolled sheet outer skin, which is deep drawn into a tray and screwed to an aluminium carrier system. Figure 5.30 shows the junction between two panels where the carrier is in four sections forming the outer and inner parts of the assembly. The aluminium skin is fixed to the outer section of the carrier, which is screwed from the inner section by a

thermal break. The inner lining is bolted back to the main structural framing.

Rain screen panels

This last type of panel is in effect a combination of rolled sheet and laminated panel in which a flat aluminium sheet 4–6 mm thick is mounted in front of a

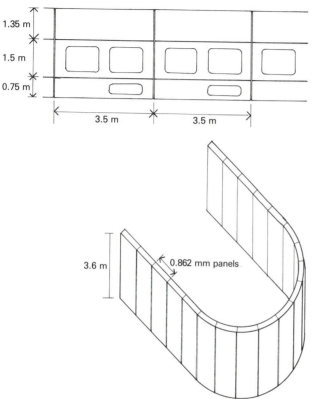

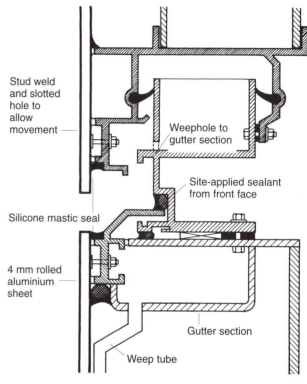

Fig. 5.28 Dimensions of panels used at Bronx Centre, New York (architect: Richard Meier).

Fig. 5.29 Horizontal joint detail from Johnson & Johnson building, New Brunswick, USA (architect: I. M. Pei).

laminated panel, itself designed for weather resistance with a ventilated cavity between the two parts of the construction. As the name 'screen' suggests, these panels are only a first-stage barrier. The panels behind provide the thermal and acoustic performance, and can be mounted into a carrier system or fixed to secondary framing in the same way as previously described. The joints between the rain screen panels should be 10 mm or more to allow for any thermal movement, and it is also advised that the fixing of the outer sheets to the carrier system should allow for

movement. The gauge of the plate panel must also be such as to avoid rippling and distortion of the sheet (in aluminium, 4–6 mm). For a further discussion of rain screen and pressure-equalized wall design, see the AAMA (1971), and Chapter 6 on curtain walling. This system of construction was used at the Umschlags AG office building in Basel (Fig. 5.31) (architects: Wetterwald and Wenger), where 1651 mm wide × 2060 mm high decorative aluminium panels were deep drawn by Schmidlin and in effect 'hooked' onto the building, with an air gap of 20–30 mm provided

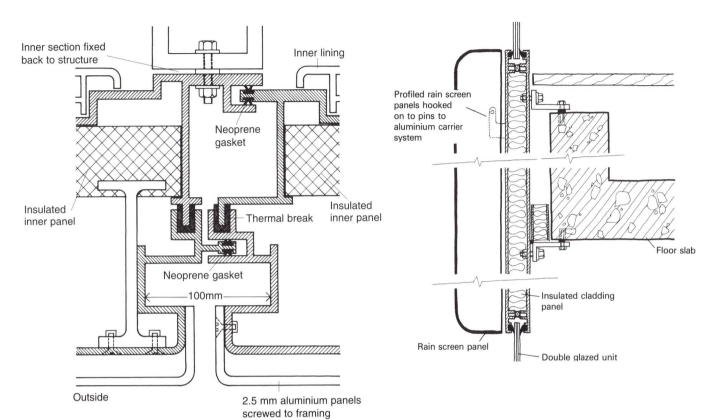

Inner section fixed
back to structure

Inner lining

Neoprene
gasket

Insulated
inner panel

Thermal break

Insulated
inner panel

Neoprene gasket

100mm

Outside

2.5 mm aluminium panels
screwed to framing

Profiled rain screen
panels hooked
on to pins to
aluminium carrier
system

Floor slab

Insulated cladding
panel

Rain screen panel

Double glazed unit

Fig. 5.30 Plan of joint between panels at Hochhaus Dresdner Bank, Frankfurt (architects: Becker, Becker and Partners).

Fig. 5.31 Section of panels used at Umschlags AG office building, Basel (architects: Wetterwald and Wenger).

between the outer panel and the insulation to ensure ventilation of the rain screen principle. Figure 5.32 shows a UK example of a rain screen, showing the air gap, the method of clipping the rain screen to the carrier, and the thermal break.

The size of the panel is limited only by the maximum size of the sheet metal panel and its ability to span between supports. However, the outside face of the inner laminated panel must also be waterproof, and this may limit the size of the overall assembly if joints in this panel are to be avoided. Rain screen

panel principles have also been developed for over-cladding using metal panels mounted onto concrete block back-up walls.

These metal panels (usually powder-coated aluminium) are fixed to supporting mullions fixed in turn back to the external building fabric. A cavity is usually formed between the original and the new fabric, which is insulated, normally with mineral fibre insulation. Panels are normally locked to the supporting mullions by stainless steel pins, either exposed or secret fixed, with the joint forming a rain screen mounted on brackets fixed to the blockwork or brickwork wall behind (Fig. 5.33).

The Knowsley fire in Liverpool (Bolland, 1991) raised questions on fire spreading through cavities within this type of assembly, and the need for fire stops at floor levels and around window openings. There is an essential conflict between the need for horizontal fire stops and the provision of ventilated cavities.

Fire tests on board products being undertaken at Cardington (BRE, 1989) indicate that some benefits of fire spread may result from reducing the width of the cavity, but clearly the amount of air movement to ensure proper ventilation of the system to avoid condensation will need to be checked.

The situation of wind loading on the inner face of the cavity is also not clear. Work by N. J. Cook (Building Research Establishment) on dynamic wind effects on board products with open joints has shown that fluctuations in wind pressure are transmitted through open joints to act directly on the original wall. Manufacturers should be asked to confirm their assumptions on wind loading when specifying the fixings and type of back-up wall.

Finishes

As well as the organic coatings normally associated with profiled metal claddings, such as Plastisol PVC finishes and PVF_2 coatings, manufacturers will offer a number of alternative finishes, such as:

- electrostatic powder coating;
- anodizing;
- thin premium paint coatings;
- vitreous enamelling;
- stainless steel.

Electrostatic powder coating

Powder coating is the application of thermo-hardening polyester/polyurethane within an air oven. This process has to be carried out in the factory, and it is therefore necessary to coat matching flashings and trims. Cured coating thickness should not be less than 75 μm.

Anodizing

Advantage can be taken of the oxidation characteristics of aluminium to provide an anodized aluminium finish (Fig. 5.34).

There are essentially three types of anodizing. The first two are **natural anodizing** (silver) and **two-stage anodizing** (bronze colours – the best known example in the UK is Anolok). Both these types of anodizing use sulphuric acid electrolyte to produce an initial silver-coloured anodic film. In the case of silver anodizing this is then sealed. In two-stage anodizing, the film is dyed in a second stage and sealed to give the required shade.

Sulphuric acid produces a relatively coarse-grained pore structure, which is not as resistant to abrasion as the structure produced by **integral anodizing** (golds, bronzes, greys and blacks). This is a one-stage process in which the colour is produced by the alloying constituents in the parent metal combined with the action of proprietary acids (e.g. Kalcolor, Duranodic, Calanodic) and then sealed. This produces a dense anodic film with superior weathering characteristics and resistance to abrasion. Thus, although silver anodizing is produced in one stage by the action of electrolyte on the metal, it does not have the film density of the true integral anodizing using sulphosalicylic type acids, and it is normally recommended that this type of anodizing should be washed down more frequently than the other types.

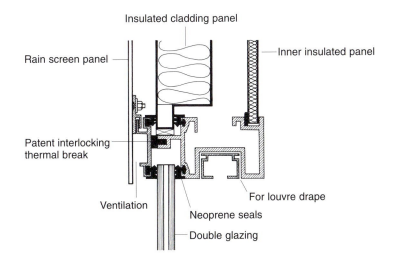

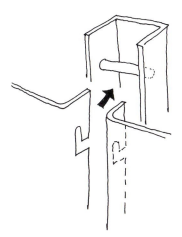

Fig. 5.32 Typical rain screen detail (section).

Fig. 5.33 Typical secret fixing using metal pins for rain screen cladding.

Fig. 5.34 Typical anodizing bath.

Fig. 5.35 Panels for Gatwick Airport on Duranar coating line.

Anodizing should be carried out using alloys specifically suited for the process according to BS 3987 : 1974. The minimum required anodic film thickness is 25 μm for external applications.

The European Wrought Aluminium Association (EWAA, 1978) specification for anodizing types includes a terminology of aluminium anodizing procedures. Anodized aluminium panels will need washing down regularly to avoid pitting of the surface, and thus provision of cleaning rails and cradles should be allowed for.

One difficulty is that it is extremely difficult to match the colour of anodizing, which is dependent on the time the panel is in the electrolyte and the type of alloy used. Although it is possible to agree upper and lower limits of colour variation with the manufacturer, some variation must inevitably be accepted, depending upon the degree of quality control in the factory.

Thin premium paint coatings

It is this difficulty of maintaining anodizing quality that led to some American architects expressing a preference for more recent paint finishes, such as fluoropolymer coatings (e.g. Duranar from PPG Industries), or acrylic finishes.

These premium, thin (20 μm) paint films are dependent for their performance on the type of substrate used, and, as with all organic coating, long-term durability will be affected by the type of metal pre-treatment used.

Figure 5.35 shows panels for Gatwick Airport being coated with 3 coat Duranar finish.

Vitreous enamelling

Vitreous enamelling is normally associated with steel panels, because it is difficult to ensure proper adherence of the enamel to aluminium sheeting. The zero carbon steel necessary for the manufacture of vitreous enamelled panels is available in widths of up to 1520 mm, which can restrict the size of the finished panel (Fig. 5.36).

Stainless steel

Stainless steel can also be used for external cladding. For laminate sheets, in which the integral strength of the core allows the use of thinner gauge metal skin, the cost of the stainless steel may not be significantly more than the equivalent stiffness gauge of aluminium with a hard anodic anodizing. The surface finish of stainless steel can vary from a matt descaled finish to a bright, highly polished finish. The choice depends on the use and the cleaning technique to be applied. Number 4 dull polished finish, which is not highly reflective, is suitable for most architectural applications, because it combines ease of cleaning with uniformity of appearance.

Proprietary systems and their fixing

The size of box panels is often governed by the type of press used to produce the box tray. Steel panels produced for the Patera system (Fig. 5.37) were stamped out in three separate pressings for the same panel prior to fabrication into a composite unit using a mineral wool insulation core.

The type of metal used can also influence the maximum size of the panel. Stainless steel, for exam-

Fig. 5.36 Vitreous enamelling of panels at Escol Ltd.

Fig. 5.37 Patera building systems using panels 3.6 m × 1.2 m (courtesy of Patera Products Ltd).

ple, is available from BSC (Stainless) Sheffield in coils up to 1520 mm wide. Similarly, zero-carbon flattened steel, necessary for the manufacture of vitreous enamelled panels, is available in widths up to 1520 mm. Consequently, the size of vitreous enamelled panels is normally restricted in size to 2950 mm × 1450 mm allowing for flange dimension. Panels can of course be assembled into a larger assembly using supporting framing: for example, façade units 3.86 m wide × 4.42 m high at Burne House Telecommunications Centre, London, were made up from panels less than 1 m wide mounted into a steel channel cladding frame. The construction incorporates a vapour barrier and a conventional inner lining. As well as 'one-off' designs for specific projects, a number of proprietary panel systems are marketed in the UK using box-type construction with both steel and aluminium metal skins. For details of these systems see Brookes and Stacey (1990).

Several early Russian examples of box-type composite panels and their joints are shown in Fig. 5.38. Experience in the use of composite panels in New Zealand is also reported by Sharman and Duncan (1980).

In the same way as some allowance must be made for thermal expansion using sheet metals, similarly for box-type panels consideration must be made for possible thermal movement, particularly when using aluminium. Simple calculation shows that if the interior panel temperature varies by 20 °C, then for a 1200 mm wide panel with a steel skin (coefficient of linear thermal expansion approximately 12×10^{-6}°C) the width will vary by 1 mm. An aluminium skin would move twice this amount. Thermal movement is normally allowed for at the joint, and if an overlap H-shaped aluminium extrusion is used, then the legs of the H-section should be long enough to accommodate this movement. It is not good practice to 'gun in' a sealant into these sections to provide a final seal, as this can be squeezed out onto the face of the panel because of thermal movement (Sharman and Duncan, 1980). Vertical movement of the panels must also be allowed for in the design of any top and bottom fixings. Allowance for movement must be made in the panel fixing (Fig. 5.39).

Aspect II

The joining and fixing of metal composite panels is critical to their performance in use. Additional stiffness can often be achieved by the incorporation of UPVC edge profiles, which also act as joint formers to achieve more complex jointing and fixings and to allow interchangeability with other components, such as doors, windows and louvres.

The search for an improved four-way crossover junction without the use of ladder gaskets (as used for the Sainsbury Arts Centre, University of East Anglia and Gatwick North Piers), and the need to avoid the use of site-applied sealants, were fundamental design aims in the design of the new cladding system, Aspect II, developed by Brookes Stacey Randall Fursdon, and

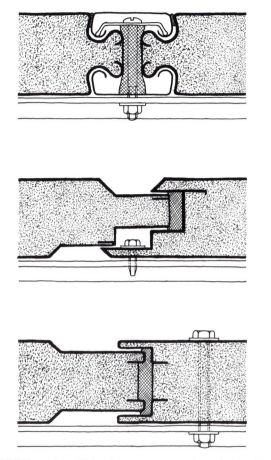

Fig. 5.38 Examples of joints between composite units developed in the former Soviet Union.

Fig. 5.39 Proprietary patent fixing device.

now manufactured and marketed by Coseley Panel Products (Fig. 5.40).

This system of interchangeable façade components offers the opportunity of rearranging or adapting the building envelope at any stage during the construction process or after the building is occupied. Aspect II allows panels to be interchanged with glazed panels, louvres or doors. Even loading bay doors can

be relocated. For a full description of the development of the system, see Anon (1990).

Aspect II achieves the freedom of movement of the components of the building envelope as suggested by the architects of the Hertfordshire Schools Programme in 1948: 'the freedom of movement of a queen on a chessboard as opposed to the limitations of a pawn' (Fig. 5.41). Modular coordination is essential to make this possible.

Fig. 5.40 Interchangeable façade panels.

The method of fixing panels is to fix via an aluminium clamping plate located within the UPVC edge profiles and behind the primary gaskets. The clamping plates are secured with a stainless steel countersunk socket-head machine screw to a rear fixing block, which slides within the vertical rear aluminium carrier. The Aspect II system is entirely secretly fixed, and avoids any problems of aligning fixings, sealing fixings or panel damage by fixings.

The panels can be easily assembled or disman-

tled by a skilled fixing team. The clamping plate has been carefully engineered with allowance for thermal movement, rotational effects and tolerance. The interface of the clamping plate and the UPVC edge section has been designed to minimize thermal bowing of the panel. The number of clamping plates is dependent upon the wind loading and panel size.

In Aspect II the weatherseal is formed by the primary gasket framing the perimeter of the panel. The inner seal is formed by a horizontal airseal mounted to the top and bottom edges of the panel. This is clamped against the vertical airseal mounted to the rear aluminium carrier. A still air zone exists between the primary gaskets and the airseals. Drainage continuity is maintained using sealed joints in the rear carrier, normally at 4 m centres, which allow for thermal expansion. The sill detail is designed to drain moisture from within the assembly to the outside.

All components, including windows, louvres and doors, have a common method of jointing, and are secretly fixed. This achieves a system of coordinated components, through their means of jointing, resulting in a coherent assembly of diverse elements. Throughout these elements the finish can be common or highly varied depending on the needs of each project and the requirements of the specifying architect.

The sequence of assembly starts with the aluminium rear carriers, which are fixed back onto the building's substructure and aligned, plumbed and shimmed to a flat plane. The fixings and shims will be determined by the nature and tolerance of the substructure of each project. The vertical airseals are rolled into the locating channels in the front face of the carriers. These airseals run continuously up the elevation, and initially are oversized to allow for shrinkage (Fig. 5.43).

The first panel, complete with its horizontal airseal and primary framed gasket, is offered up to the carrier and restrained by bolting down the aluminium cladding plate onto the aluminium rear block within the carrier. The clamping plate is then partially backed off and the adjacent panel offered up to the carrier. The joint between the panels is compressed to 15 mm. (Fig. 5.44). The panel alignment is checked. The action of tightening the clamping plates' socket-head machine screws compresses the panel and the horizontal airseals against the vertical airseals. It is good practice to assemble a bay of panels vertically.

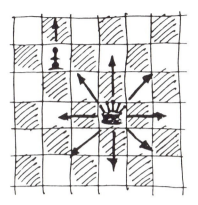

What seems to be required of the structure is something analogous to the freedom of movement of a queen on a chessboard as opposed to the limitations of a pawn.

Fig. 5.41 Hertfordshire chess diagram.

Fig. 5.42 Panels face fixed using Allen key, then tightened to a specific torque.

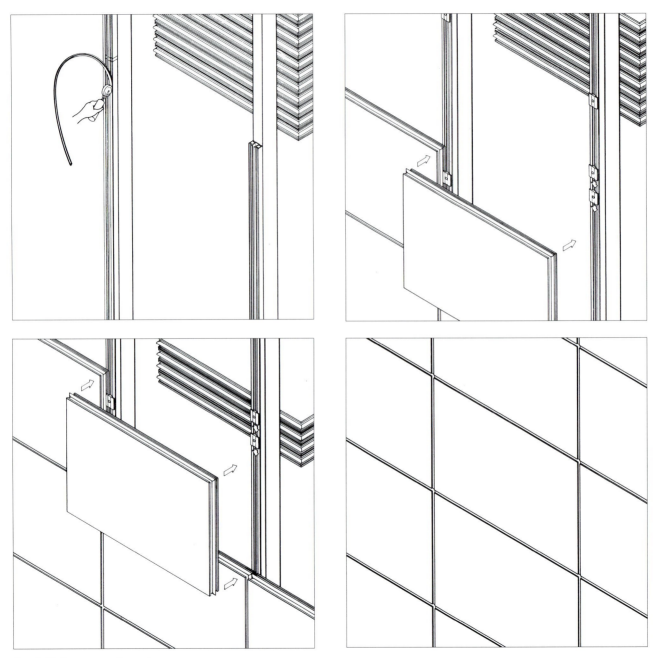

Fig. 5.43 Sequence of erection.

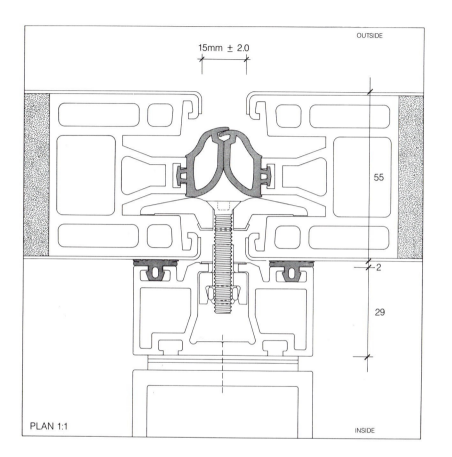

Fig. 5.44 Part of joint.

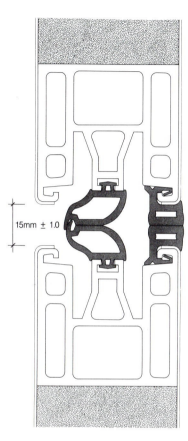

Fig. 5.45 Section through horizontal joint.

The weatherseal of the horizontal panel-to-panel joint is formed by the primary framed gaskets, backed up by the panel-mounted horizontal airseals. There is no requirement for horizontal rear carriers or sub-frames (Fig. 5.45).

To minimize thermal migration, the rear clamping block of the clamp plate assembly has an extended nose section. This ensures that panels are retained within the gridlines of the panel modules. The assembly is restrained vertically by stop blocks, which are

located in every third horizontal panel joint and carry dead load.

In order to extend the spanning capabilities of the louvre and window sections, increasing the maximum performance to 3.6 m clear span at 1.6 kN/m^2 wind loading, horizontal wind stiffeners have been designed (and patented) by Brookes Stacey Randall Fursdon. An example of one of the more unusual designs shown (Fig. 5.46) comprises two aluminium extrusions. One forms the beam, which is profiled and has holes cut

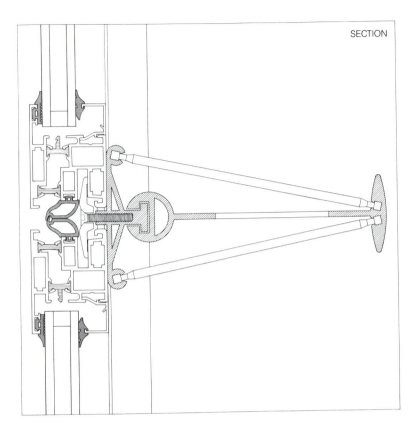

SECTION

Fig. 5.46 Horizontal wind stiffener.

in the web. Depending upon the structural performance required, these holes can change in diameter and shape. The second extrusion forms discrete 60 mm wide brackets fixed into the panel joint at typically 900 mm centres. These two extrusions are linked by 6 mm diameter stainless steel struts.

The composite construction of Aspect II can use various core insulation materials to achieve U values of 0.45 – 0.35 W/m²°C.

The Aspect II system of panels and its associated components were produced after a design, research and development programme of mock-ups, prototypes and testing. The panel-to-panel joint, with its patented framed gaskets, has been tested at BSI according to BS 5368 Parts 1–3 for air penetration, weather resistance and wind loading.

The system is in 1996 under development by Coseley Panel Systems, who are responsible for its manufacture and installation. Quality control during production is important to ensure the panel's performance in use (Fig. 5.47).

Fig. 5.47 Quality control during production.

References and further reading

AAMA (1971) *Aluminum curtain walls, rain screen principles and pressure equalized wall design. Design details of three recent buildings.* Architectural Aluminum Manufacturers Association, Chicago.

Alan Brookes Associates (1992) Ebor ASPECT II brochure, London.

Anon (1990) Design by cooperation – metal panel cladding. *Architects' Journal*, **191** (4), 61–65.

Becker, W. E. (1968) *US Sandwich Panel Manufacturing Marketing Guide*, Technomic, Stamford, CT.

Bolland, S. (1991) Liverpool blaze raises cladding safety alarm. *Building*, **256** (7692), 7.

BRE (1989) *External walls, combustible external plastics insulation, horizontal fire barriers*, DAS 131, May, Building Research Establishment, Garston.

Brookes, A. J. (1983) *Cladding of Buildings*, Construction Press, London.

Brookes, A. J. (1985) *Concepts in Cladding*, Construction Press/Longmans, London and New York.

Brookes, A. J. (1991) Composite metal panels, design and manufacture. *Architects' Journal*, **194** (12), 53–56.

Brookes, A. J. and Grech, C. (1990) *Building Envelope*, Butterworth-Heinemann, London.

Brookes, A. J. and Grech, C. (1992) *Connections*, Butterworth-Heinemann, London.

Brookes, A. J. and Stacey, M. S. (1990) Product review – cladding. AJ Focus, *Architects' Journal*, March.

Brookes, A. J. and Stacey, M. (1991) Cladding – product review. AJ Focus, *Architects' Journal*, July, 29–50.

Brookes, A. J. and Stacey, M. (1992) Cladding – product review. AJ Focus, *Architects' Journal*, October, 25–32.

Brookes, A. J. and Stacey, M. (1993) Cladding – product review. AJ Focus, *Architects' Journal*, December, 15–25.

EWAA (1978) *Specification for the Quality Sign for Anodic Oxidation Coatings on Wrought Aluminium for Architectural Purposes*, European Wrought Aluminium Association, June.

Foster, N. (1978) Frontiers of design (lecture), in *Norman Foster. Foster Associates* (ed. I. Lambot), Watermark, Hong Kong, Vol. 2, p. 127.

Huber, B. and Steinegger, J. C. (1971) *Jean Prouvé*, Les Editions d'Architecture Artemis, Zurich.

Murphy, J. (1978) Skin deep, technics for external wall panels. *Progressive Architecture*, **2**, 83–91.

Sharman, W. R. and Duncan, J. R. (1980) *Building material usage in primary processing industry buildings.* Building Research Association of New Zealand Technical Paper, October, p. 30.

Thorogood, R. (1979) *Metal Skinned Sandwich Panels for External Walls*, BRE CP6/79, Building Research Establishment, Garston.

6

Curtain walling – glazing systems

Definition

Curtain walling may be defined as being non-loadbearing walls, usually suspended in front of a structural frame, their own deadweight and wind loadings being transferred to the structural frame through anchorage points. Usually they consist of a rectangular grid of vertical or horizontal framing with infill panels of glass or some other lightweight panel, but that is not always so, for the term 'curtain walling' encompasses a wide variety of systems (Fig. 6.1):

– patent glazing;
– pressed or extruded metal box framing;
– suspended glass assemblies;
– silicone-bonded glazing.

There are a number of proprietary systems available for each of these types, as described below.

Patent glazing

Nineteenth-century Victorian glasshouses gave many opportunities for the development of dry assembly systems of glass and metal (Fig. 6.2). Many of these are shown by Hix (1995) in his excellent historical study of glasshouse construction. Joseph Paxton's Crystal Palace had wooden glazing bars made on site by sophisticated milling machines, but by the time it was moved to Sydenham it was largely rebuilt using metal glazing bars

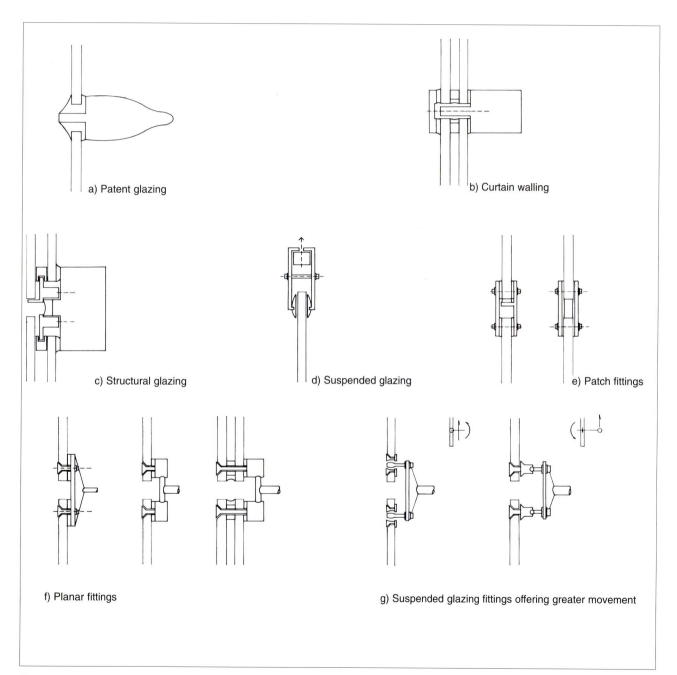

a) Patent glazing

b) Curtain walling

c) Structural glazing

d) Suspended glazing

e) Patch fittings

f) Planar fittings

g) Suspended glazing fittings offering greater movement

Fig. 6.1 Development of glazing systems.

and a puttyless glazing system, the recognized advantage of which was illustrated by the abundance of patents taken out at that time (hence 'patent glazing'). Sections of the nineteenth-century patent glazing bars are shown in Guedes (1979). It was the necessity to provide good natural lighting in factories, using north light roof construction in the 1920s and 1930s, that really promoted the commercial development of the large number of types of patent glazing sections used today (Fig. 6.3). Modern patent glazing systems for both inclined and vertical applications were shown in Patent Glazing Conference (1980); however, more recently this type of glazing support has fallen out of favour, mainly because of inherent difficulties with thermal breaks and the availability of more sophisticated forms of curtain walling.

Metal box framing

The term 'curtain walling' is most commonly associated with a rectangular grid of vertical and horizontal frame members, introduced from America during the 1950s mainly for use in high-rise office buildings (Hunt, 1958).

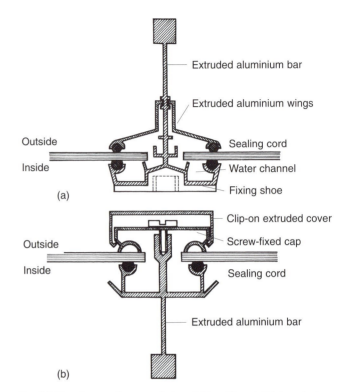

Fig. 6.3 Two forms of patent glazing: (a) traditional; (b) inverted.

Two buildings in particular helped the popular aesthetic approval of the framed curtain wall: the United Nations Secretariat (architects: Harrison and others, 1947–50) and Lever House (architects: Skidmore, Owings and Merrill, 1952), both in New York. Important forerunners of these were buildings such as the Gropius factory at Alfeld (1911), the Bauhaus, Dessau (1925–26) and Le Corbusier's Maison Suisse at the Cité Université, Paris (1930–32).

There are two basic approaches to assembling a box-framed curtain wall (Fig. 6.4). Either:

—   the component parts of the system are assembled on site, with panels being offered up to a

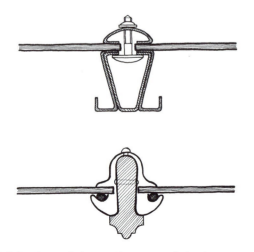

Fig. 6.2 Sections of nineteenth-century glazing bars.

frame (sometimes known as the 'stick' system); or
—   the panel system is bolted together, the panels
     themselves becoming the frame.

Both systems have the advantages associated with
a high degree of prefabrication; the first method has
more easily handled components, but site construction
time may be longer.

Means of support

The means of support and the layering of the arrange-
ment can totally change the appearance of the façade.
There is clearly an interest in providing diversity in the
means of support for a particular project to reduce
the visual bulk of the supporting framework or to
achieve a particular span requirement. At the YKK M&E
Centre in Japan by Roy Fleetwood, the two-storey curtain walling of the ground floor is supported by a transom and mullion of a similar section. However, the
mullions are stiffened by the use of a pin-jointed lattice
truss. This truss mullion, a combination of cast and
extruded aluminium, was developed by YKK Architectural Products (Fig. 6.5).

A similar structural approach has been taken by
Bentham Crouwel in their extension to Schiphol Airport in The Netherlands, where once again a consistent mullion and transom box is supported by a
vertical truss. However, with the truss, the architects
have opted for a curved vierendeel beam, very similar to that designed for Stansted Airport (Fig. 6.6).

The curtain walling designed for the British Air-
ways Combined Operations Centre (developer Lynton
for Heathrow Airport) by Nicholas Grimshaw & Partners demonstrates the potential of extruded sections,
which are more visually interesting than a simple box
section and capable of accepting many functions that
interact with the building envelope. This is achieved
by a family of extruded components (Fig. 6.7).

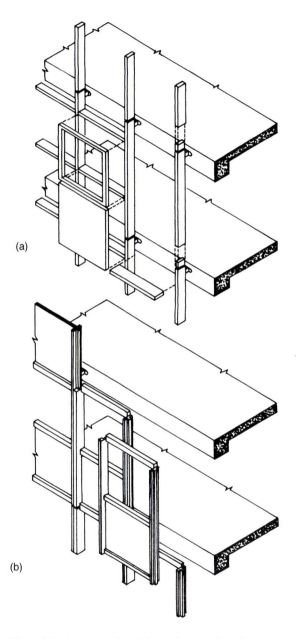

(a)

(b)

Fig. 6.4 Basic forms of curtain walling construction:
(a) stick system; (b) panel system.

Fig. 6.5 YKK M&E Centre in Japan by Roy Fleetwood.

Fig. 6.6 Glazed wall at Stansted Airport (architects: Foster Associates).

Renzo Piano, when designing a curtain walling system for Alucasa of Milan, Italy, used cast aluminium sections, which, when bolted together, acted as wind bracing between floors, replacing the traditional box extrusion (Fig. 6.8).

Typical spans

In metal box framing, the window mullions are the principal members of the grid; horizontal members rarely form the support for curtain walls. Vertical members spanning from floor to floor must withstand axial stresses caused by self-weight and bending caused by wind loads, and it is in this direction that the mullion must have greatest stiffness and strength, a principle also illustrated by the 'fin' section of a patent glazing bar. The depth of the mullion is thus dependent upon its span and the area of glazing it is required to support (module spacing). Prouvé illustrated as early as

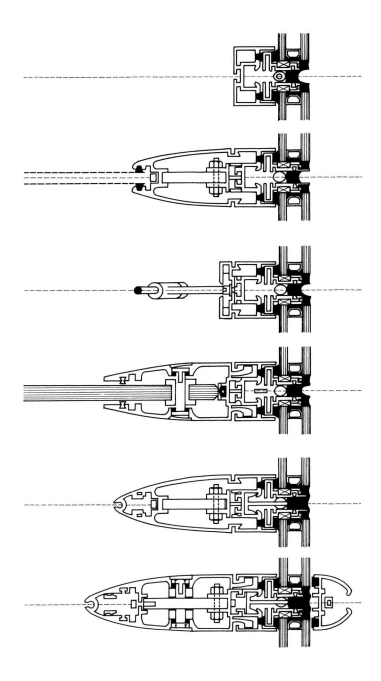

the 1930s how the use of a range of proprietary sections could cope with a variety of spans (Fig. 6.9).

The size of the curtain wall grid is determined by the costs of the vertical members, the section size being weighed alongside the number of members required. Proprietary systems offer a module size of between 760 mm and 1200 mm, and according to Elder (1977), where mullion spacings are over 1200 mm, glass costs and mullion sizes increase considerably.

It may be that, with the introduction of designs of glazing systems for particular projects rather than for general use, the sections can be engineered for larger mullion spacings. Float and sheet glasses are now available for use with these larger grid dimensions. Information on maximum sizes normally available for glasses used in curtain walling can be obtained from the various glass manufacturers, including Pilkington Bros, St Helens. BS 6262 : 1982 *Code of practice glazing for buildings* also gives information on design considerations affecting spanning characteristics of different types of glass.

Joints and connections

The logic underlying the frequency at which prefabricated curtain walling elements are jointed together can be summarized in terms of manageability (both in transportation and in site handling) and reduction of movement per joint, particularly thermal, in the system and between the system and the supporting framework.

Joints to allow thermal movement

The framing members of the curtain wall, which are fixed back at points to the supporting structure, must be allowed to contract and expand freely with changes of temperature. Rostron (1964) shows various methods

Fig. 6.7 Mullion section for BA Combined Operations Centre by Nicholas Grimshaw & Partners.

Fig. 6.8 Cast aluminium truss for 'Alucasa' System by Renzo Piano.

of allowing for thermal movement (Figs 6.10 and 6.11) between the framing and structure using sliding joints. Reduction and friction at sliding connections is provided by slotted holes and plastic washers.

It is also essential to provide some kind of discontinuity in the frame itself. Frequent jointing within the frame will reduce the thermal movement per joint in the system and between the system and the main structure. There are essentially three types of such joints:

- slip joints;
- butt joints between solid mullions and transoms;
- spring connections between adjacent panels.

Both Rostron (1964) and Schaal (1961) illustrate examples of such joints. Slip joints in vertical framing members, using a loose spigot or a swaged offset, are shown in Fig. 6.12.

Figure 6.13 illustrates the principle of a slip joint

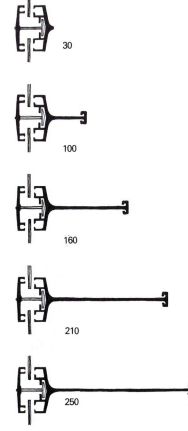

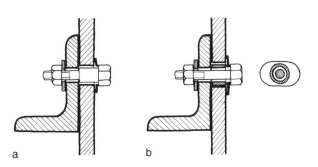

Fig. 6.10 Reduction of friction at sliding connections by using slotted holes and plastic washers and: (a) shoulder bolts; (b) sleeves and standard bolts (from Rostron, 1964).

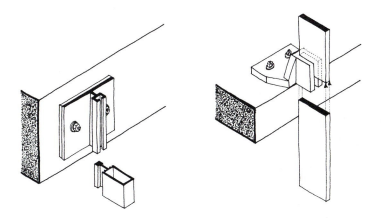

Fig. 6.9 Range of sections (depth) to cope with a variety of spaces.

Fig. 6.11 Allowance for thermal movement in methods of fixing (from Rostron, 1964).

in a split mullion, where the male and female sections permit thermal movement between the frames.

Butt splicing between solid mullions and transoms allows a joint thermal movement (Fig. 6.14). Examples of spring joints are shown in Figure 6.15. Flexible metal closure strips can also be used.

Weatherproof joints

Joints between frame and infill panels take the form of beads, gaskets and sealants. The following requirements must be met.

– Joints should be wind- and rainproof (if the inside of the infill panel is sensitive to moisture, the edges should be protected).
– Self-weight of panels and wind loads should be transferred evenly to the frame.
– Panels and framing members should be free to

expand and contract independently (if subject to movement; thermal or structural).

- Joints must allow for dimensional and alignment variations between shop and site.

Rostron (1964) describes two main types of joints, open and closed:

- Open joints allow water to enter the joint, control its passage and provide drainage.
- Closed joints form a completely weatherproof barrier.

Open joints have several advantages: they easily accommodate movement, erection is quick, and subsequent maintenance of joint seals is reduced. However, the joint profile tends to be more complicated, and closed joints are more commonly used sealed with either rigid or flexible seals.

Rostron (1964) also defines two main classes of joint shape: integral and accessory.

- In integral joints, members are shaped in such a way that bringing them together forms the joint.
- Accessory joints require additional parts to form the joint.

Each of these joint shapes has three principal forms (Fig. 6.16). The choice of joint shape is determined by requirements for tolerance in assembly, movement, sequence of assembly, performance factors and aesthetics.

The component nature of curtain walling means that there are many joints in the envelope. These joints, at frequent intervals, are necessary to enable components to be of manageable dimensions. Frequent jointing will also reduce the problem of thermal movement per joint. Recent years have seen the development of

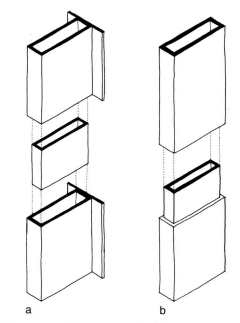

Fig. 6.12 Two types of slip joint in vertical framing members (based on Rostron, 1964): (a) loose spigot or sleeve; (b) swaged offset.

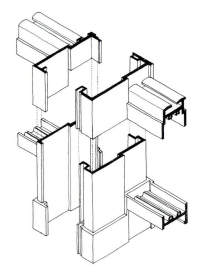

Fig. 6.13 Slip joints in split mullions (based on Schaal, 1961).

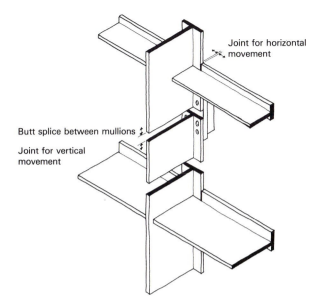

Joint for horizontal movement

Butt splice between mullions

Joint for vertical movement

Fig. 6.14 Butt joints between solid mullions and transoms (based on Schaal, 1961).

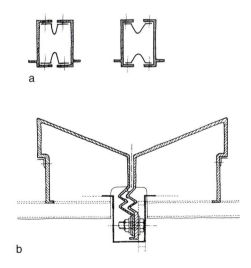

a

b

Fig. 6.15 Spring connections (based on Schaal, 1961): (a) flexible metal closures in the joints; (b) example of a spring joint.

more sophisticated joints moving away from metal and mastic joints between panels towards patent neoprene gasket designs. Neoprene also helps to accommodate thermal movement between the panel and its framing.

Joints between glass and frame

When glass is the infilling panel the edge cover given to the panel at the joint has to be limited in order to avoid too great a temperature differential occurring between the edge and the exposed surface, which may lead to the glass breaking. Stroud, Foster and Harington (1976) (pp. 170–171) recommend that the edge cover to the glass should be limited to 10 mm, although a dark-coloured frame will alleviate the problem of thermal stressing. A more detailed discussion of glass fracture is contained in T. A. Schwartz's paper to the Second International Conference on the Durability of Building Materials, 1981 (Schwartz, 1981), in which he advises designers to consider the strength-degrading effects of long-term loads, environment and surface defects as part of their glass selection process. At the same conference Zarghamee and Schwartz (1981) reported on a study designed to discover causes for the loss of metal edge bands from insulating glass units during service. Such studies have been carried out as a result of experience with glazing units that have failed either by seal fracture or by glass fracture due to cyclic movement between the glass and the curtain wall. The most dramatic example is that of the Hancock Tower in Boston, where it is necessary to stabilize the main frame in order to reduce the amount of movement.

Edge clearance

Edge clearance should take account of the thickness, strength and spanning capacity of the glass, its deflection, its thermal movement and the condition of the edge of the glass (edge fracture). It is also necessary to take into consideration the strength of the supporting member, its deflection, its thermal movement and the type and characteristics of the weatherseal. The possible creep under dead load and characteristics and correct placement of the setting block must also be taken into consideration.

Some glass manufacturers will offer general guidance, such as the rule of thumb that 'designed edge cover should equal the thickness of the glazing', and most of their recommendations hover around this general principle.

The received opinion from persons within the curtain walling industry is that it is normal that recommendations for minimum edge cover be quoted as **guidance for design**. In setting the measurable minimum to be achieved on site, safety factors should also allow for the particular conditions of use and geometric complexity of the project under consideration.

Some individual manufacturers carry out tests on typical assemblies to take account of variations that occur in practice and any reduction in performance (weathering or strength) that could thus occur. Schuco, for example, in their FW50 curtain walling advise 12 mm as minimum (measured) edge cover governed by the width of the rear airseal.

The Architectural Aluminum Manufacturers' Association Guide 1979, p. 100, Table C, recommends 9/16 in edge cover for 9/16 in glass.

The relevant British Standards include:

– BS 952 : Part 1 : 1978 *Glass for glazing. Classification*
– BS 6262 : 1982 *Glazing for buildings*
– BS 5516 : 1991 *Design and installation of sloping and vertical patent glazing*
– BS 8000 Part 7 : 1991 *Workmanship on building sites.* These are vague and open to interpretation on the issue of recommended edge cover.
– BS 952 gives description and availability of differ-

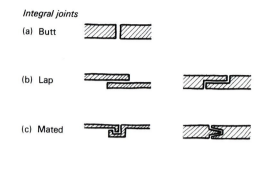

Integral joints
(a) Butt
(b) Lap
(c) Mated

Accessory joints
(a) Spline
(b) Cover
(c) Frame and stop

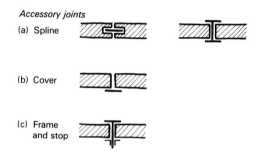

Fig. 6.16 Integral and accessory joints (based on Rostron, 1964).

ent types of glass – no recommendations are given on edge thickness.
– BS 6262 Table 14 gives guidance on minimum edge cover for single glass exceeding 6 mm thickness. For 12 mm thick glass, this would require an edge cover of 9 mm.

There is no specific clause with recommendations for edge cover to toughened curved single glazing in BS 5516 : 1991, although interestingly it is accepted in this standard that solid plastic glazing will not necessarily be assembled centrally within the supporting framing, and 15 mm minimum cover is given for the worst case of edge cover (p.60, Fig. 8) for plastic glazing.

In clause 10.8.1 of BS 5516, a minimum edge cover of 7 mm is used as a basis of the calculation for minimum thickness of glazing taking account of 3 second gust wind load (dynamic load). This value of edge cover has been used as a basis of the subsequent charts for predicting glass thickness contained in the standard. According to Dr Bowler-Reid, one of the authors of the standard, the value of 7 mm was a 'guesstimate' based on the experience of the various members of the standard committee and using calculations provided 'on a conservative basis' by Pilkingtons.

This figure may be taken as a design value based on common experience. It does not necessarily reflect a detailed amount of possible future movement due to vibration, temperature changes or deflection of the glass, which may not be restrained on all four edges.

Insulation and cold bridging

The thermal performance of the assembly is largely determined by the insulating properties of the infilling panel. The nature of the frame, does, however, have some influence upon performance. If the frame is made of metal and is unprotected from the external environment, then it will set up a cold-bridging pathway. The effect can be overcome by discontinuity in the framing members using a patent plastic thermal break (Fig. 6.17). In some systems the metal frame is continuously protected from external conditions by a neoprene gasket, and in this way cold bridging is avoided. If the frame is constructed from timber members then no problems of cold bridging arise.

Fire resistance

A curtain wall has to be regarded as an unprotected area in relation to the transmission of fire to adjoining property. The extent to which an unprotected area is permitted by the fire provisions of the Building Regulations

Fig. 6.17 Patent plastic thermal break.

or, if applicable, the London By-Laws is determined by the distance to the wall from the relevant boundary. A common method of reducing the unprotected area, which is acceptable under both sets of regulations, is to provide a non-combustible back-up wall, usually of masonry construction, 100 mm from the inner face of the infill panel. This approach does, however, invalidate certain advantages of a curtain wall installation, such as saving floor space and light loading of the primary structure.

Suspended glass assemblies

Suspended glass assemblies using glass as the load-carrying material were first developed with Foster Associ-

Fig. 6.18 Willis Faber Dumas at Ipswich.

ates in 1973 for the Willis, Faber and Dumas Insurance building in Ipswich (Fig. 6.18). The system consists of two glass components: a **wall skin** formed from sheets for 12 mm toughened glass (armour plate) and **vertical fins** fixed perpendicularly to the skin to provide lateral resistance to wind loads. These are formed from 19 mm armour plate.

The system is constructed from the top down. The topmost glass panels are independently suspended from the main structure using one central bolt, the load

being spread across the width of the glass by means of a top clamping strip. Figure 6.19 shows the original sketch of the fixing back to the concrete structure at the head of the assembly.

Subsequent panels are hung from those above using 165 mm square brass patch connectors with stainless steel fixing screws. The height of the assembly is limited by the shear strength of the bolt holes that are drilled through the glass, the maximum height being 23 m.

At Ipswich, the glass fin to resist wind loads is fixed back to the floor structure. Because the wall skin is suspended, the glass expands downwards. In order to allow vertical movement between the wall and the fin, the inside patch connector comes in two parts, one for attachment to the fin and the other to the façade (Fig. 6.20). The two parts dovetail together, allowing the fins and façade to slide vertically independently of one another.

The early design of the dovetail, as shown in the Pilkington design guide (Pilkington, 1975), included a square dovetail, which allowed the two parts of the fins to separate under horizontal movement. Later versions used a rounded sleeve dovetail (Fig. 6.20). At the base of the assembly, a channel section is fitted, which supports the glass laterally and has sufficient depth to accommodate the cumulative downward expansion of the façade.

Joints between the glass are totally exposed to the weather, and rely for their efficiency solely on the properties of the silicone-based sealant and the correctness of its application.

The whole system was designed to be capable of accommodating errors in the concrete frame of 50 mm in any direction.

Within ten years Pilkington had reduced the means of securing toughened glass to a flush countersunk machine screw fitting. This fitting, known as Planar,

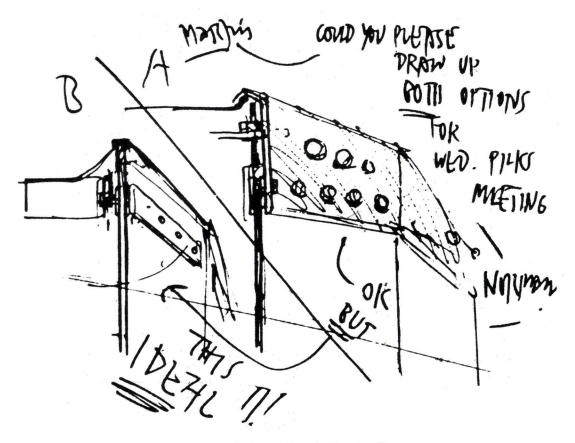

Fig. 6.19 Original sketch of clamping strip at head of assembly at Willis Faber Dumas.

was first used on Briarcliff House, Farnborough, by Arup Associates and at the Renault Centre by Foster Associates (Fig. 6.21), where 4 m × 1.8 m glazing was restrained using 'spider' connections back to the horizontal steel framing at 1.33 m centres (Fig. 6.22). Later, the span between fittings was increased at Lime Street Station, Liverpool, where 1.95 m × 1.05 m glazing was fixed back to a vertical steel framing at 1.95 m centres (Fig. 6.23 a and b). Generally, a rule of thumb is that Planar fittings should be connected on a grid of

pick-up points approximately 2 m square in order to reduce the deflections between the fittings. Fittings for double glazing typically comprising 10 mm outer toughened glass, 16 mm air space and 6 mm inner toughened glass were first used on the Porsche UK Headquarters, Reading, by Dewhurst Haslam Partnership in the form of 4° rooflights.

Later (1989) developments in reducing the number of supports for suspended glazing included East Croydon Station by Brookes Stacey Randall Fursdon

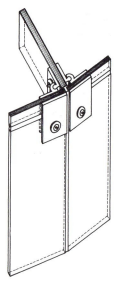

Fig. 6.20 Attachment between glass fin and façade at Willis Faber Dumas.

Fig. 6.21 Renault Centre glazing.

(Fig. 6.24), where cast stainless steel outriggers are used to reduce the effective span of the glass between fittings. Thus the span of the 12 mm toughened glass is reduced from 3000 mm to 2400 mm.

The vertical mast is held at its head and base by stainless steel castings with an articulated head detail, to accommodate the vertical and differential movement between the structure and the vertical cladding (Fig. 6.25). The 10 mm clear toughened glass roof glazing is suspended below stainless steel twin armed castings using 902 mark 2 Planar fittings (Figs 6.26, 6.27).

Other elegant solutions for the problem of picking up the four bolts for the fittings include Nicholas Grimshaw's stainless steel 'dinner plates' at the Financial Times Print Works (Fig. 6.28) and Mark Goldstein's aluminium bronze cast brackets for 111 Lots Road in London.

A refined support system for suspended glazing

is the stainless steel wire wind bracing developed for the Parc de la Villette in Paris by Rice, Francis and Ritchie, for Adrien Fainsiber in 1986, where a special detail allowed a span between the main structure of 8 m square, and enabled flexing of the wire-braced intermediate structure and also alignment of the glass (Figs 6.29, 6.30).

There is now (1996) an increasing diversity of supply of countersunk and plate patch fittings. As well as the Pilkington Planar fitting these would include countersunk fittings by Greenburg UK, Marcus Summers UK, MAG Design & Build UK, Seele in Germany, Eckelt in Austria and GME in Belgium (Fig. 6.31).

At the Montmartre funicular transport station project in Paris, Groupe ALTO developed a new countersunk fitting in conjunction with the manufacturers, SIV. This has a 48 mm face diameter, compared with the 28 mm diameter of the Planar fitting. The 12 mm

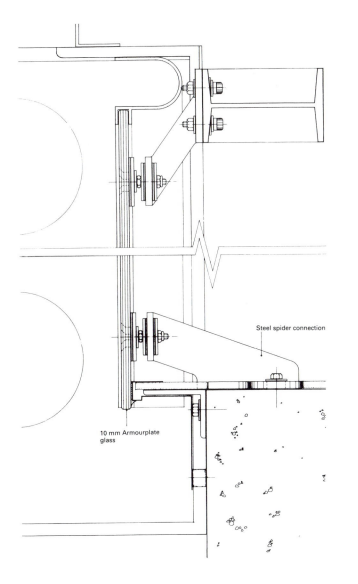

10 mm Armourplate glass

Steel spider connection

Fig. 6.22 Detail of glazing fitting at Renault.

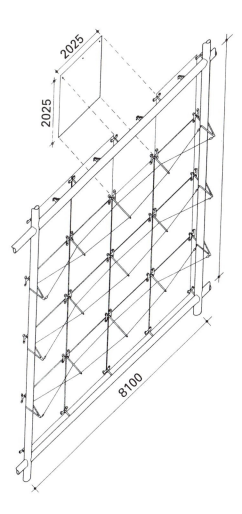

2025

2025

8100

Fig. 6.23a Spans of glazing at Parc de la Villette.

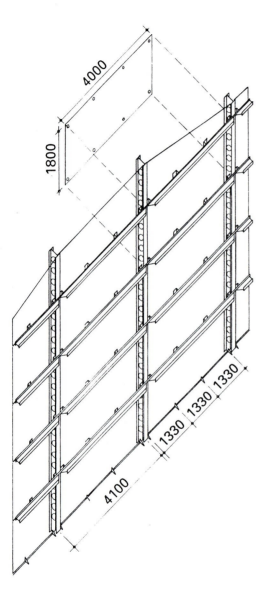

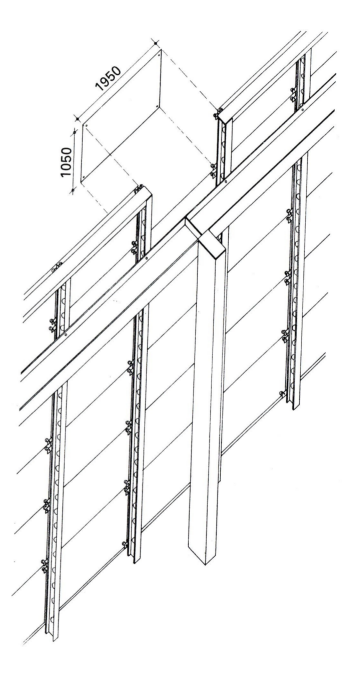

Fig. 6.23b (contd.) Spans of glazing at Renault (left), and Liverpool Street (right).

Fig. 6.24 East Croydon Station.

Fig. 6.25 Detail at head of glazing.

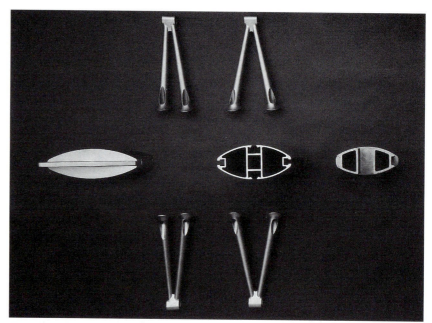

Fig. 6.26 Cast stainless steel outriggers.

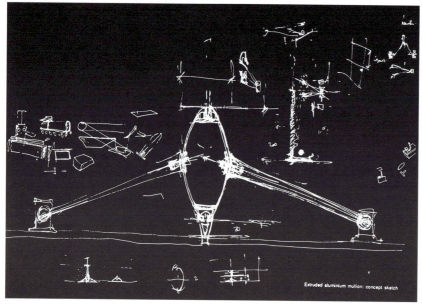

Fig. 6.27 Plan detail of glazing at East Croydon Station.

Fig. 6.28 Financial Times glazing.

Fig. 6.28a Suspended glazing at Financial Times Building, London (architects: Nicholas Grimshaw & Partners).

plus 8 mm laminated glass (not toughened) provides canopies in which the glass is moulded to the desired radius and the fittings are able to accept 22° of rotation (Fig. 6.32).

In most cases the span of the supporting framework is one or two storeys, but at the Reina Sofia Museum of Modern Art in Madrid (architect: Ian Ritchie) the entire glass envelope to each 36 m high tower is suspended by stainless steel rods from roof level. Here, each panel of glass is individually supported. The size of each panel is determined by wind load, economic glass thickness, structural module and heights between floors. Each 12 mm thick pane of toughened glass is 2966 mm wide by 1833 mm high and is suspended from one central panel fitting on its top edge (Fig. 6.33). Flush Planar fittings at each corner provide fixing points for the wind bracing system.

It is noticeable on some projects using suspended glazing that many four-way joints, each nominally 10 mm, are misaligned. Manufacturers are helping to improve this by reducing acceptable variations of the

Fig. 6.30 Parc de la Villette structure support of glazing.

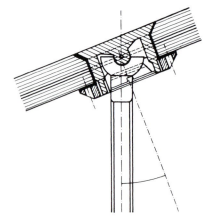

Fig. 6.29 Detail of Parc de la Villette glazing.

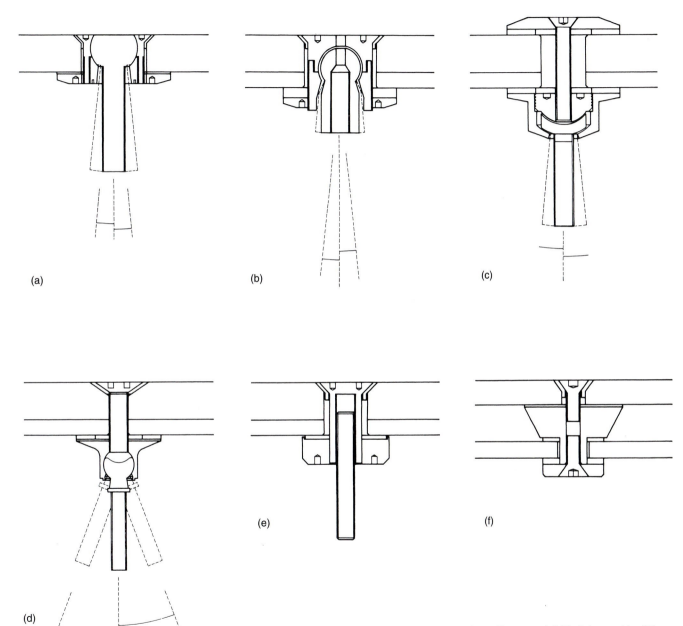

Fig. 6.31 Variants from Planar and RFR fittings with different degrees of movement: (a) Marcus Summers, UK; (b) GME, Belgium; (c) Seele, Germany; (d) Eckelt, Austria; (e) Eckelt; (f) MAG Design & Build, UK.

Fig. 6.32 Curved laminated glass used at Montmartre funicular.

glass size and increasing the accuracy of drilling the countersunk holes. This is being achieved by investment in new automated machinery, which has the added facility of polishing edges.

The maximum available size of glass for use with the Planar system is limited by the need for the glass to be toughened. The toughening process of pre-stressing the skins by heating them to 620 °C followed by controlled cooling increases the load capacity of the glass. The maximum size available therefore depends on the size of the toughening ovens at St Helens. The present maximum size for clear toughened glass is 4.2 m × 2.1 m. Some European glass-makers have larger or different aspect ratio ovens and so there is the opportunity for Pilkington to collaborate with them or invest in larger ovens also. Pilkington can combine Planar with body tinted glasses, reflective glasses, double glazing, low-emissivity coatings and even the screen printing of dots or frettings. All these additional processes influence the maximum size.

Of all the types of cladding discussed in this book, suspended glazing and structural glazing are undergoing the fastest development in the application of new systems and environmental control.

Silicone-bonded glazing

Throughout Europe, the past 10 years have seen a considerable growth and development in the use of structural glazing, predominantly to form the non-loadbearing glass envelope of major building projects.

The end walls of the Sainsbury Centre, UEA (Fig. 6.34), installed by Clark Eaton in 1976, remain one of the most elegantly and minimally detailed assemblies of clear annealed glass, 15 mm thick, stiffened by 25 mm, 600 mm wide, full-height glass fins. When Solaglass replaced two units, owing to their size, 2.5 m × 7.5 m, they could only be supplied as 15 mm annealed glass by Saint-Roch of Belgium, edge finished by Solaglas in Coventry. The maximum size of toughened glass is primarily governed by the toughening oven. Pilkington's current maximum size for toughened glass is 4.2 m × 2.1 m. Where larger sizes are required, Plyglass can offer laminated glass up to 6 m × 3.2 m.

It is interesting to note how under BS 6262 : 1982 it would not have been possible to have replicated the end wall of the Sainsbury Centre, as the standard would have required the first 800 mm from ground level to be toughened or laminated glass. Requirements have changed since its issue, and on 1 June 1992 the revised Building Regulations' Section N: Glazing Materials and Protection was introduced. This specifically recognizes the strength characteristics of annealed glass; it is in effect a relaxation of the

Fig. 6.33 Suspended glazing at Reina Sofia Museum, Madrid.

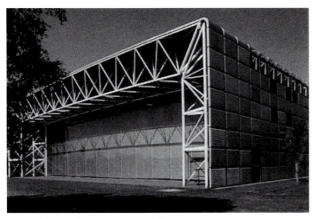

Fig. 6.34 Sainsbury Centre glazing.

Fig. 6.35 Sculpture Pavilion, Sonsbeck (architects: Benthem and Crouwel).

requirements of BS 6262. Diagram 2 states the size of annealed glass that can now be used. At 15 mm thick the panel size is not limited by Section N, and the end walls of the Sainsbury Centre are once again a legitimate solution for a building in England and Wales. However, one must remember that annealed glass is not tolerant to local stress build-up of a loadbearing bolted fitting.

The façade glazing of the Sainsbury Centre is restrained against wind suction by a continuous vertical silicone seal only (Adshead Ratcliffe AR1081 translucent). It is designed to withstand wind loads up to 1400 N/m². Overall, the glass is retained by a glazing channel set flush with finished floor level and fin boxes at the head of the glazing, which are fixed back to the main structure via slotted holes to accommodate tolerance and movement.

In contrast, many current assemblies opt to back up the silicone seal by using a mechanical patch plate or a countersunk fitting. The success of fittings such as Pilkington's Planar has encouraged their use in glass fin assemblies, where it is questionable if in fact they are necessary.

More recent applications of silicone-bonded glazing that have caught architects' imagination include the Sculpture Pavilion at Sonsbeck, The Netherlands, by Benthem & Crouwel Architekten. This pavilion is a direct development of the earlier relocatable house for Jan Benthem in Almere (Brookes and Grech, 1990, p.5). By taking the idea of structural glazing even further, this pavilion is a totally glazed 24 m long, 6.2 m wide, 3.65 m high transparent box (Fig. 6.35). Unfortunately, the museum was designed as a temporary building, and has now been dismantled. A similar proposal was developed by the Faculty of Architecture (course leader Ulrich Knaak) for a pavilion at Aachen University (Fig. 6.36). Such proposals, offering maximum transparency through the use of large sheets of glass and minimizing the apparent means of support, have been adopted almost as a style of architecture identified with the 1990s. Brookes Stacey Randall Fursdon's use of curved toughened glass and cast stainless steel fittings at the Thames Water Tower, London (Anon, 1996), led the judges of the RIBA Awards 1995 to comment: 'Such is the inspirational nature of

Fig. 6.36 Pavilion at Aachen Faculty of Architecture.

Fig. 6.37 Detail of Thames Water Tower, London (architects: Brookes Stacey Randall Fursdon).

the tower that the panel felt its qualities transcended the question – is this sculpture or architecture?' (Fig. 6.37).

Glass

Finally a few words on the glass itself. There are now many forms of glass and glazing available to provide environmental control and thermal performance. These include:

- variable-transmission glazing;
- liquid crystal laminates;
- electrochromatic glass;
- low-emissivity coatings;
- transparent insulation;
- screen-printed glazing;
- fixed shading systems.

These are described in detail by Brookes and Stacey (1992), pp. 29–41. Also, Button and Pye (1995) summarize much useful technical information.

The weakening effects of nickel sulphide inclusions in glass have been the source of much debate. Annealed glass is unaffected, but in toughened glass spontaneous fracture may occur in use, because of the expansion of the unstable nickel sulphide as it changes phase over time. It is not practical to detect these inclusions by a non-destructive process. However, heat soaking can be carried out after toughening. This is a destructive quality control procedure, as panes with inclusions will shatter during the soaking process, but it is an essential specification requirement.

At present there is no standard method for heat soaking, but contrary to rumour there should be no detrimental effects, and it should not reduce the compressive stress within the glass below a specified level. There is no applied symbol to indicate that glass has been heat-soak treated and, as the Glass and Glazing Federation points out, you cannot visually inspect for heat soaking. It is therefore important that the current Kitemark should be modified to identify when a toughened panel has been heat-soak treated.

In applications where thermal shock is considered a potential risk, but the strength of toughened glass is not required, it is possible to specify a heat-strengthened glass, as it has approximately twice the mechanical and thermal strength of annealed glass.

Research into improving the thermal performance of double-glazed units continues. It is now possible to specify a double-glazed unit which has low-E coatings on surfaces 2 and 3 with a gas-filled cavity between to achieve a U value of 1.1 W/m²°C. Pilkington and BASF have together been carrying out research into a granular aerogel, which provides a transparent insulation layer achieving U values between 0.5 and 1 W/m²°C. This is now supplied by Flachglas of Germany, a Pilkington subsidiary.

Photovoltaic glass, recently considered only an experimental technique, is rapidly becoming a cost-effective option, but it has yet to be seen integrated into a major building façade.

Finally, developments in laminated toughened glass have allowed engineers and architects such as engineer Robert Nijsse, working with architects Kraayvanger Urbis on their own offices in Rotterdam, to build an all-glass bridge using a combination of 10 mm clear toughened glass, PVB laminate and 6 mm Eco-plus low-E glass for the walls and two layers of 15 mm toughened glass bonded with a PVB laminate to form the floor (project architect: Dirk Jan Postel). This is an interesting example of collaboration between engineer, architect and fabricator. Having produced this all-glass bridge, Robert Nijsse believes 'it would now be possible to make just a glass tube without the supporting beams' (Fig. 6.38). The challenges of the next generation of suspended and structural glazing are enormous.

Fig. 6.38 Laminated toughened glass as used at the glass bridge in Rotterdam by engineer Robert Nijsse.

References and further reading

Anon (1996) Glass pavilion at Aachen and Thames Tower, Barometer, London. Glasforum, 19-21.

Brookes, A.J. and Grech C. (1996) *The Building Envelope and Connections*, Architectural Press.

Brookes, A.J. and Stacey, M. (1992) Product Review - Glazing and Curtain Walling. AJ Focus, *Architects' Journal*, July.

Brookes, A.J. and Stacey, M. (1993) Product Review - Glazing and Curtain Walling. AJ Focus, *Architects' Journal*, September.

Brookes, A.J. and Stacey, M. (1994) Product Review - Glazing and Curtain Walling. AJ Focus, *Architects' Journal*, November.

Button, D. and Pye, D. 'Glass in Architecture', Butterworths, 1995.

Crawford, D. (1974) 'Design opportunities in patent glazing', The Architect, Dec. 1974, pp. 48-50.

Elder, A.J. (1977) The A.J. Handbook of Building Enclosure, Architectural Press: London, pp. 151-6.

Frohnsdorff, G. (1981) Proceedings of the second international conference on the durability of building materials and components, 14-16.9.81, National Bureau of Standards, Gaithersburg, Maryland, USA.

Guedes, P. (1979) Encyclopaedia of Architecture and Technological Change, 'Glazing systems', Macmillan: London, p. 284.

Hix, J. (1995) The Glass House, MIT: Cambridge, Mass., USA.

Hunt W.D. (1958) The Contemporary Curtain Wall - Its Design Fabrication and Erection, F.W. Dodge Corporation: New York.

Patent Glazing Conference (1978) Patent glazing - Guidance Notes to BS 5516, PGC: Epsom, Surrey, March 1978.

Patent Glazing Conference (1980) Patent glazing, product selection and specification. Architects' Journal, 172 (49), 1103–1117 (reprints available from PGC, 13, Upper High Street, Epsom Surrey).

Pilkington (1975) Armourplate Suspended Glass Assemblies, Pilkington design guide, Pilkington Bros, Ltd, St Helens, Merseyside, Sept 1978.

Rostron, M. (1964) Light Cladding of Buildings, Architectural Press: London.

Schaal, R. (1961) Curtain Walls - Design Manual, Reinhold: New York.

Stacey, M. 'Products Development - Maximum Vision' Architects' Journal, Focus Edition, October 1988.

Stroud, Foster and Harington (1979) 'Cladding - curtain walling'. Mitchells Building Construction Structure and Fabric, 2nd edn, Part 2, Batsford: London, pp. 167–175.

Index

Aachen Faculty of Architecture 173
Acoustic performance 73, 104
Accessory joints 158
Acrylics 100
Adhesives 128
Aero Club Roland Garros 113
Aggregate finishes 33
Air currents 7
Air seals 7, 28
Airstream caravan 113-114
'Alucobond' 127-129
Alucasa System 154
Aluminium steel (aluzine) 100
American Express Building Brighton, 53
Anmac Ltd 46-47
Anodising 136
Anolock 136
Aramid fibre 39
Architectural Aluminium Manufacturers' Associations (AAMA) 6-7
Arne Jacobsen, Dissing and Weitling 127
Armshire Reinforced Plastics, 41
Ash and Lacey 93
Aspect II 141-145

BA Continued Operations Centre 153

Baffle grooves 28
Baffle strips 27
Barcol test 43
Bead polystyrene 126
Becker, Becker and Partners 135
Bentham & Crouwel 151,172
Blaga 47
Blemishes 43
Boat construction 42
Booth-Murie Ltd 118
Brensal Plastics 47
Briggs Amasco 118
British Alcan 93
Bofil R 10
Brockhouse Lightform 116
Bronx Centre, New York 132,134
Brunel Centre, Swindon 88
Butt joints 157

Calonodic 136
Canadian National Research Council 132, 134
Capillary action 5
Carbon fibres 38
Cartridge fasteners 108
Castle Park, Nottingham 42
Catalyst 37
Cem-Fil 66
Central Electricity Generating Board (CEGB) 93
Chopped strand mat 38

City-Corp, New York 132
Cladding, definition of 89
Closed joints 156
Coating line 95
Cold bridging 159
Colour matching 97-100
Compatibility 106
Composite metal panels 115
Conatus panels 116
Condensation 48
Constrado 89
Contact process 39
Continuous foaming line 123
Continous strand mat 38
Coseley Panel Products 141
Cours conceptions construction 113
Covent Garden Market, London 41
Cover strips 78
Crédit Lyonnaise, London 66
Curing 37
Curtain walling 148
Curved panels 127

Danish Embassy, London 127
'Deep drawing' techniques 87
Delamination 130-131
Decking 89
Deflection 103
Density 73

Diespecker Marble 12
Durability 97
Durability, International
    Conference of 101
Duranar 138-139

E Glass 38
East Croydon Station 5 161-162
EPDM 54
Electrostatic powder coating 136
End laps 109
Escol Ltd 139
European Wrought Aluminium
    Association 138

Face-up and face-down castings
    18-19
Farrell and Grimshaw 50
Federal Reserve Bank, Boston 133
Fibreglass Ltd 45
Financial Times 91, 162, 167
Fire-retardant additives 45
Fire performance 71
Fire resistance 45, 159
Fixings 30-32, 59, 105
Flash line 42
Flashings 109
Fleetwood, R 151
Floclad 93
Flour City 132
Fluoropolymers (PVF$_2$) 100
Fluting 96
Foamed polyurethane panels 120
Foster Associates 92, 117, 118,
    119, 159

Galvanizing (hot-dipped) 94
Gartner, Josef and Co 125, 132

Gaskets 54-56, 76-78, 159
Gatwick North Piers 121
Gel coat 40
Gillingham Marina 45
GRP moulds 41
Glass fibre reinforcement 37
Glass 175
Gravity 5
Grimshaw, Nicholas, Partnership
    42, 50, 51, 151

Hancock Tower, Boston 157
Handling on site 20, 80, 103
Heathrow Eurolounge 80
Height of stacks 105
Hermann Miller factory, Bath 50,
    56, 59
HMS Raleigh 56, 60
Hochhaus Dresdner Bank,
    Frankfurt 135
Honeycomb paper core 126,
    120
Horizontal profiled cladding 109
Horizontal support ribs 23
Hunter Douglas 118

IBM offices, Greenford 92
Impact tests 103
Impermeable coatings 70
Indulex Engineering Company 44
Installation of profiled sheeting
    103
Insulation cores 120
Integral anodizing 136
Inverted glazing bars 150

Johnson and Johnson building,
    New Brunswick 134

Joints in curtain walling 153

Kalcolor 136
Kevlar 39
Kinetic energy 5

Laminated panels 124
Landmark Tower, London see
    Thames Water Tower
Lateral proofing 96
Lattice gaskets 121
Lever House, New York 150
Leyland and Birmingham Rubber
    Co 118
Liner trays 110
London Docklands Corporation
    12
Loose spigot 154
'Luxalon' panels 118

Majumdar, A.J. 65
Manual spraying 67
Master Patterns 41
Mastic sealants 25
Mechanised spraying 67
Meier, Richard 132
Melrose Centre, Milton Keynes 69
Metakaolin 70
Metal box framing 150-159
Metal Roof Deck Association 94
Metal stamping 86
Montmatre Funicular 162
Montreal Protocol 123
Monocoque shells 113
Menier Chocolate Factory 3
Method of Building, Property
    Services Agency (PSA) 13,
    93

Milton Keynes Kiln Farm factory
    86
Mineral wool 110, 120
Modern Art Glass 127
Moisture movement 73, 78
Mondial House, London 46, 59, 61
Monsanto 'House of the Future' 3
Moulds
    adjustable 14
    for concrete 117-119
    for GRP 41

National Exhibition Centre 80
Neoprene see Gaskets
'Nip' rollers 125
Nijsse, Robert 175

'Oil canning' effect 131
Olivetti factory, Haslemere 49
Open-drained joints 26, 78
Open joints 156
Organic coatings 97
Oxford Regional Hospital Board
    system 116-117
Outram, J 12

Paint coatings 100-101
Parc de la Vilette 162, 163
Patent glazing 148
Patent Glazing Conference 150
'Patera' system 139-140
Paxton, Joseph 148
Pei, I.M. 134
Perfrisa panels 118
Phenolic foram 68
Piano and Rogers 65
Piano, R. 113, 154
Pigments 47, 70

Pilkington Bros. 153, 160
Plastisol 101, 136
Platternpress 125
Polyester resin 37
Polyisocyanurate foam 121
Polymerization 37
Polyurethane core 68, 120
Polystyrene 120, 68
Portland cement 69
Press
    braking 85
    moulding 39
Proprietary systems 139
Pressure-equalized wall design 6-7
Prouvé, J. 113
Property Services Agency (PSA)
    Method of Building 93, 89
PTFE 79
Pultrusion 41

Quality control 42-43

Rain screen panels 133
Reina Sofia Museum 171
Release agents 39
Renault Centre 118, 121, 122
Repair on site 81
Resin-injected techniques 39, 41
Ribbed construction 62
Rice, P. 34-35
Richard J. Hughes complex, New
    Jersey 132
Riven slate 49
Roll form line 95
Rolled sheet panels 131-133
Rovings 38
Royal Arsenal Co-op 76
Safe temperature ranges 105

Sainsbury Centre, University of
    East Anglia 117-121, 171
Sandwich construction 76
Scicon factory, Milton Keynes 76
Scott Bader Ltd 37
Secret fixings for rainscreens 137
Segmentation 6
Self-tapping screws 107
Shaped profiles 51
Sheeting rails 110
Shrinkage 41
Side laps 109
Silicone bonded glazing 171
Single-skin construction 73
Sinosoidal profiles 89, 91
Site vulcanising 118
Slip joints 154
Sliwa, Jan 116
South Eastern Architect's
    Consortium (SFAC) 116
Spacer jigs 105
Split moulds 42
Spray-dewater process 68
Spray lay up 41
Spring connectors 157
Standardization 45, 14, 116
Stainless steel 139
Stansted Airport 108, 152
Steel Construction Institute 89
Steel moulds 117
Stiffening ribs 130
Stirling, James 49
Stubbins, Hugh 132, 133
Stud Frame System 74
Superform metals 117
Surface
    tension 5
    treatments 69

Surfactants 123
Suspended glass assemblies 159-171
Swaged offset 156
Swiss Aluminium Co. Ltd 127

Tapered profiled sheets 93
Teeside Polytechnic 58
Textured moulds 33, 49
Thermal
    breaks 159
    expansion 58, 105
    stressing 131
Tilting moulds 19, 42
Timber moulds 17
Tolerances 19, 105, 109
Tooling 41

Trent Concrete 10
Top hat sections 54
Trapezoidal profiles 89, 93

Ultraviolet
    light 56, 57
    stabilisers 47
Umschlags AG office, Basel 135
United Nations Secretariat 150
UOP Fragrances factory 77

Vacuum
    forming 41
    pressing 125-126
Vertical glass fins 160
Vertical foaming 24
Vertical strengthening ribs 24
Vitreous enamelling 139

Water Research Centre 48-49
Weathering 33
Web thickness 23
Weep holes and tubes 29, 30
Willis, Faber and Dumas, Ipswich 161
Wind loading 136
Winwick Quay, Warrington 51

Xenoc arc test 48

Yarsley Laboratories 47
YKK M&E Centre 152

Zero carbon steel 139
Zinc coatings 101